In *Hope Wins*, Leisa shares her struggles and breakthroughs in raising a child with special needs. Her vulnerability and down-to-earth approach provide the reader with a sense of the very real pressures and raw emotions experienced, but also some very practical answers to help enjoy the journey.

As Leisa, Ian and Justin's pastor, it has been my privilege to see a large component of this story unfold and to witness their uncompromising faith in Jesus through the highs and lows. This story is not over. There are still hills to climb. But the faithfulness of God rings true. The One who has made a way where there seemed to be no way, and the One who has given strength, grace and wisdom will continue to see them through. That is why we can boldly proclaim: "Hope Wins!"

—**Ps. Jon Cathie**
Senior Pastor, Capital Edge Church, Canberra

Leisa is a modern-day pioneer, paving the way for carers of special needs children. It hasn't been easy for this woman of courage who has weathered many storms to achieve hard-fought outcomes on behalf of all the parents out there who feel that they don't have a voice. Leisa has embraced the abilities of her special needs child, and this is her family story.

—**Jenny Haines**
Retired Carer Support Coordinator, Victoria

An open, honest and sometimes raw look into the life of a parent dealing with the challenges of raising a special needs child. A must-read for all special needs families.

—**Andrew Bliesner**
Brother, brother in-law and uncle of Leisa, Ian and Justin, UK

As a physician who treats children and adolescents with various disabilities, I value the knowledge and insight that Leisa offers in this book. Her firsthand experience as a parent adds invaluable help to those who are seeking solutions to their special needs families. I highly recommend this book to parents who are seeking better ways to manage their special needs families. For those who feel that they are already doing a splendid job, this book will further sharpen and deepen your existing skills. It is a book I like to have on my book shelf!

—**Dr Kam Wong**
Child and Adolescent Psychiatrist, Sydney

Reading Leisa's insightful story, *Hope Wins*, a common thread stood out for me: The need for **H**aving **O**ther **P**eople **E**ngage. That's what helps the individual and families of those with disabilities and gives them hope. It is not a solo journey; it really does take a group of people who care 'a whole awful lot'. It's those individuals that can become the hands and feet of Jesus Christ in the lives of families who often feel isolated, alone and hopeless.

—**Helen Buckley**
Live Like U Matter Counselling, Canberra

Raising a special needs child is difficult. In *Hope Wins*, Leisa openly and honestly shares her journey through the trials, challenges, and triumphs that she and her family have faced in caring for and raising Justin. Leisa vulnerably shares the reality of being misunderstood, feeling judged, and the desperation of simply wanting to give up. But the fact that is she did not give up, and learning how she triumphed makes this book a must-read. Fabulously practical, and penned with hard-fought wisdom, this book is written with an authority that comes only when an individual has faced and overcome considerable adversity. Leisa's engaging story provides powerful hope that with Christ, regardless of the adversity we face, victory is possible for those who remain deeply connected to a Holy God!

—Paul Ryan
Centre Director, Ellel Ministries, Sydney

Hope Wins

Torn Curtain Publishing
Wellington, New Zealand
www.torncurtainpublishing.com

© Copyright 2021 Leisa Williams. All rights reserved.
ISBN Softcover 978-0-6451757-0-7

No portion of this book may be reproduced, stored in a retrieval system or transmitted in any form or by any means—electronic, mechanical, photocopy, recording or otherwise—except for brief quotations in printed reviews of promotion, without prior written permission from the author.

All details included in this book are written from the author's best recollection and perspective. Names of people included in this book are used with permission. Some names and places have been changed to preserve anonymity. This book is not intended as a substitute for professional counselling or medical advice.

Unless otherwise noted, all scripture is taken from the Holy Bible, New International Version®, NIV®. Copyright © 1973, 1978, 1984, 2011 by Biblica, Inc.™ Used by permission of Zondervan. All rights reserved worldwide.

Cataloguing in Publishing Data
    Title: Hope Wins
    Author: Leisa Williams
    Subjects: Special needs, Family life, Christian living
    Typeset in Palatino Linotype

A copy of this title is held at the National Library of Australia.

Hope Wins

Overcoming Feelings of Hopelessness
in Special Needs Families

LEISA WILLIAMS

To Ian,

my loyal and loving husband.

Throughout this book, the words 'special needs' have been used to describe a person with disability. The author acknowledges that other language can be used and that the intention should always be to see the person before the disability, or the ability within the disability.

Contents

Introduction	15
PART ONE — SETTING THE SCENE	19
Chapter 1 A Meaningful Life	21
Chapter 2 Dealing with Grief and Transition	33
Chapter 3 The Danger of Self-Pity	43
Chapter 4 The Importance of Self-care	51
Chapter 5 Combatting Stress	61
Chapter 6 The Benefits of Pets	69
PART TWO — MOVING FORWARD	79
Chapter 7 Getting from Here to There	81
Chapter 8 How to Become Unstuck	95
Chapter 9 Grit & Determination	103
Chapter 10 Grappling with Injustice	111
Chapter 11 Managing Time, Finances and Holidays	121
PART THREE — CULTIVATING A HOPE-FILLED LIFE	129
Chapter 12 Learning to Trust	131
Chapter 13 Travelling the Pathway to Hope	143
Chapter 14 Hope Wins	149
AUTHOR'S NOTE	159
ACKNOWLEDGEMENTS	161

Introduction

Unless someone like you cares a whole awful lot, nothing is going to get better. It's not.

— 'The Lorax' by Dr. Seuss

In addition to my husband, this book is dedicated to all those who care 'a whole awful lot.' These words from Dr. Seuss's book, The Lorax, often ring in my head. I am forever grateful to all those who have cared 'a whole awful lot,' for without these people in our lives, our family might not have gotten better. This is why I am sharing my story with you. I do not share it lightly; I share because I care 'a whole awful lot' about the pressures that special needs families experience and desire to offer hope in what others may consider to be hopeless situations.

Perhaps you are battling caregiver fatigue due to the additional responsibilities that come with caring for a special needs child. Maybe you are serving as a familial caregiver as a result of an accident, trauma, mental illness, or aging. Perhaps you have friends in this situation and feel helpless in knowing how to provide support in difficult circumstances. The insights offered in this book are for each of you.

I am writing mostly from the perspective of being a parent to a special needs child, but I believe what I have to say will resonate with anyone dealing with ongoing difficult circumstances. May my story give you hope and inspiration, especially if you are a parent of a special needs child. We all love our children and want the very best for them, and yet as carers it is easy for our own needs to be neglected. If you wish to remain connected and engaged in life and live the life for which you are purposed, or if you are a parent who wants to flourish and thrive and not merely survive in the community in which you live, this book was written to draw you out of social isolation and back into society. I desire to encourage you to put aside self-pity, embrace life, and become noticed as a person in your own right, not just by the needs in your family. I want you to discover that your life does not need to be defined by the person for whom you care and their needs. You matter and have a life that counts!

When a parent receives the diagnosis that a child has special needs, the grief and loss may be immense. For a season, the world may seem to look bleak; all the hopes and dreams held in the secret places are dashed, replaced with uncertainty. The good news is that this does not have to be the case forever. In time I came to understand that the special needs of our son were a gift that enabled me to slow down and look at my life through a different lens. But first I needed to take stock and evaluate what really mattered.

This experience can be likened to the impact Covid-19 has had on many people's lives. As this book was being written, life as we knew it was suspended due to the pandemic with people worldwide suddenly forced into isolation. The 'add-ons' of life were stripped to a bare minimum—the parties, picnics, birthdays, drinks after work, play dates with friends, trips overseas, and holidays around town effectively placed on hold to avoid the spread of the virus. Words like *social distancing* and *self-isolation* have woven their way into everyday conversations. And the reality is that lockdowns and restrictions have enabled us to focus on what is really important, rather than chasing after career opportunities, wealth, or status. Even having to iron out issues that have arisen in family relationships is a good thing. And yet, the journey can be painful. The truth is, as the mother of a now young adult son, the pandemic protocols have been eerily similar to my everyday life.

You may not have a special needs child, yet there are aspects of my story you will doubtless identify with. This book is for anyone who is wondering if they can keep going. It is for those who wonder if there is any light at the end of the tunnel—or if the tunnel even comes to an end. Every situation is unique. Perhaps your child has mental health issues that require full-time care. Chances are you are fighting not only for your child's survival, but for your own. My message to you is, don't give up. There is hope!

I don't have all the answers or claim to have 'arrived.' I will, however, share insights, tips, and encouragement from what I have learned and am learning from being the mother of a son with special needs. I invite you to journey with me as I share how I bridged the gap from a place of despair and hopelessness to one of hope and promise for the future. As you read, consider how you might use your circumstances to benefit yourself and your family relationships. How could the challenges you face help you embrace growth and healing? What would it look like to pursue what you are passionate about, rather than feeling like you are being swept along by a life that is out of control? And who will you take with you on this journey to purposeful living?

The reality is that I am here now because of two reasons. The first is because many incredible people cared for me 'a whole awful lot'. Without them, I would not have been able to persist in the face of challenging and difficult circumstances. The other reason is my faith in God which, over time, has enabled me to thrive not only as a mother, but as a teacher and now as an author, despite the storms of life.

Whatever circumstances you face, I pray that my story will help you progress from where you are now to where you want to be, and most importantly, to *who* you want to become. May you learn, even in your 'hopeless' situation, to treasure the person you are and to value the 'gold' in you.

PART 1

SETTING THE SCENE

Chapter One

A Meaningful Life

The first home we lived in was a three-bedroom house with a large deck, nestled in a garden setting that attracted native birds. How fortunate we were to have sweeping views of the Brindabella mountains, and to watch the spectacular sunrises and sunsets from our deck. Breathtaking crimsons, reds and pinks were often on display, as if a master painter had painted the sky from his palette just for our enjoyment and added soft wispy clouds knowing full well that such beauty would soothe, restore and invigorate our spirits. That beauty was a gift. Amidst the hustle and bustle of our busy lives, it allowed us to pause in wonder, to tune our senses to creation. Sometimes the colours of the sky and land were so exquisite that we would catch our breath, savour the moment, then set up the tripod to capture the sun's rays just as they captivated us. Glasses of wine, cheese and crackers, birthday cakes and barbeques all took place with a backdrop that changed like a new set design each and every day.

As much as I loved those mountains (and still do), I loved my black upright piano more. It was chunky, clunky, second-hand

and old, but its low price had made it affordable. "Can't you buy an electronic one?" Ian pleaded, "Think of the cost of tuning." I would not have a bar of it. I wanted an authentic, old-fashioned piano on which to accompany my flute students, and I got my way. I don't remember what brand the piano was, but it was mine to play and that's all that mattered. Imagining the colours of the sunsets, I wanted to use my music to recreate those spectacular images, to comfort my soul, ignite my senses, and whisk me away to a world where all my troubles were distant memories. To me, the sound of music flooding our home brought the beauty of creation indoors.

I would often envision myself playing the piano like a master, my singing filling the air as my children slept. In my mind I was playing jazz, classical and contemporary pieces, transporting myself to other places, refreshing and readying me for whatever each new day held. Music opened a door that led out of my world. It reminded me of the mural of a busy English village I had on my bedroom wall as a child. I would lie on my bed staring into the scene, pretending that I was in that scene, listening to the laughter and conversation.

My first memory of loving music is sparked by a picture of three-year-old me sitting on a small stool strumming a ukulele, my face shining as I sang, 'It's a Small World.' Dad had taught me to play the song, sitting with me to ensure that my little fingers learned the right positions. My father was a patient teacher, helping me to understand the meaning of the lines and spaces and quietly correcting my mistakes, quite unlike his aunt, who had corrected my father's mistakes with a ruler and a sharp swat each time he missed a note.

In my growing up years, music was everything to me. I remember when, as children in primary school, we were given a recorder. I was so excited that I ran through the playground after school that day squeaking out 'Hot Cross Buns' along with my classmates, not noticing that our parents were waiting outside with fingers in their ears! To me, it was glorious music.

Every week my mum used to drop me at the piano teacher's house for a lesson. When it was over, the wait for her to return often felt endless, so I turned to counting how many red cars, blue cars, and so on went past the teacher's gate before Mum arrived. I was only eight when I first played a hymn at church. It was the final song in the service, and the congregation sang along as I played the organ. Mum and Dad were so proud of me, and even more so when I went on to play my flute. Still, musically, I was a small fish in a vast pond.

That changed however, when our family moved to a small coastal town. Now I was a big fish in a small pond. All of a sudden, I was noticed! *"You have a lovely voice," "Your flute playing was just beautiful," "Would you play for our wedding?"* The compliments kept coming. I joined choirs, musicals, the school band and the community band. I went to music camps during my school holidays. I seized every opportunity that came across my path.

I pursued music passionately throughout high school, and despite not getting into my choice of music school, I ended up earning a Bachelor of Music. This required me to leave home and live in a small town eight hours away, but four years later, I graduated. Now I was a fully-fledged music teacher, though I still had not mastered the piano.

Ah, the piano. I longed to conquer its ways. Soon I had children of my own, and though they were young, I was always able to sneak in some 'me time' at the keyboard. Blissfully, I imagined myself as a master pianist, playing for two magical hours as the children slept each day after lunch. Now I had a piano of my own, tucked into a pocket in the lounge room, ever beckoning me to hone my skills, to live up to my greatest dreams.

Never could I have imagined how soon this dream would be cut short. I realise now that something changed the day, I received a call from a tearful playgroup friend. "I don't think I can help you run the group anymore," she said. I was immediately curious as to the reason. This lady was such an enthusiastic member and willingly went over and above to volunteer her time and abilities. We had spent countless hours lunching at her home and enjoying each other's company over the years. But with one abrupt phone call, that ended. Flatly, she explained that her youngest son, only twelve months old, had been diagnosed with a severe form of autism; he would never learn to speak. She was devastated to learn that her child was not developing as expected. Not only that, her oldest son had also been diagnosed with autism. She had just been told that his still-emerging speech was an attempt to mirror what others were saying, but that he had no understanding of what was being said to him. With all the therapy work to be done, her days were about to become a flurry of one appointment after another. Through her tears she told me she would be too busy with appointments to continue coming to playgroup.

I was speechless, but I silently let her go and gave her the space to do what she needed to do. A vibrant, happy mum had slipped out of sight, now travelling on a pathway foreign to the rest of us. Over the months that followed we tried to stay connected, but our lives were simply too different. I wanted to help but did not know how. I was too busy raising three children and teaching classroom music to fully grasp what had happened to her. I found refuge in my music, though it was becoming sadly obvious that none of my own children showed any signs of sharing my passion. Every day my oldest son dressed in khaki and informed me he wanted to be a soldier. My daughter had a strong love of animals. And Justin? Well, who knew what he liked? He was still a baby.

A weekend trip to visit my husband, Ian's, parents raised my first concerns. I remember Justin rolling around their loungeroom floor when Ian's mum asked, "Have you had his eyes checked? It looks like they are turning in." I had not noticed anything unusual but assured her I would follow it up, thinking it was no big deal.

The ophthalmologist wasted no time in examining our sixteen-month-old son, then informed me that he indeed had a condition known as 'strabismus' and would need to start wearing glasses. I was thrown even more when he then suggested I take Justin back to the paediatrician for a developmental check-up. He felt that Justin was not quite like other toddlers of the same age. In my mind, I presumed that the reason Justin was not yet walking was that he was simply a late developer. He loved sliding on his belly across the tiles in his sleeping bag. The truth was, he was not really crawling either. That's when it dawned on me—isn't crawling essential for brain development? We booked an appointment with the paediatrician, and trusted there would be a simple explanation.

Nothing prepared me for what was about to come. Just like my friend, I too received a call that changed everything. "Your son has developmental delays and we'd like you to bring him in for further testing."

Ian came with us to that appointment, although when he heard the diagnosis, he seemed to take it better than I did. "Justin has non-pervasive developmental delay and autism" the paediatrician said, though of course neither of us knew what that meant. Dr. Jones went on to explain that Justin would only ever have the mind of a fifteen-month-old, that he would not develop like other children, and that we needed to accept this reality. In that moment, my world as I knew it crumbled; the lid on the piano closed.

We were both speechless, though inwardly every fibre of my being screamed, "Surely something can be done." And there was something we could do—from that moment on, we could fill our days with what sounded like an unending stream of appointments, consultations and therapy sessions.

My world came to a grinding halt that day but still I resisted the diagnosis. I did not want to accept the inevitable changes that would mould and squeeze me into the agenda of caring for a child with special needs! I was spinning so many plates in the air already that I knew something would have to give; I could not keep on like I was. *But what would I give up?* My performance-oriented self was working hard to maintain composure.

I was involved in running a local playgroup, working part-time as a music teacher, teaching flute privately and participating on my church's worship team. I didn't want to quit anything. But I knew I had no choice. My time was no longer my own as I was catapulted into a schedule that included occupational therapy, physiotherapy, speech therapy, play therapy, socialisation sessions, podiatry and optometry and paediatric appointments; the list was never-ending.

Suddenly I was the mother of a special needs child. And somewhere within me, the music died.

As I took on the role of caregiver, I fought within to not lose myself, to remain who I was created to be—a vibrant, community-oriented, creative woman who wanted to remain engaged in society, connected in relationships and professionally developed in my career. But it seemed too much to expect. It seemed impossible that I could to thrive (and not just survive!) in the daunting role that had been thrust upon me. Was there any hope of a fulfilling future for my child . . . or for me?

I love my son deeply. I knew that whatever his challenges were, they were not going to stop me from doing what needed to be done to enable him to flourish. And so, as I started down this new path, I made a deliberate choice to lay down everything in my life except classroom teaching and playgroup, in order to enable him and my other family members to thrive.

Nothing in me wanted to accept the inevitable changes that would mould and squeeze me into the agenda of caring for a child with special needs. However, those words rang true, "Unless someone like you cares a whole awful lot, nothing is going to get better. It's not." Now, that person was me! I needed to manage 'a whole awful lot' and accept the care of people who cared for us 'a whole awful lot'. But with the care came fatigue, loss of self and even confusion of direction. My life soon became enmeshed with my son's life.

For a while, we managed to keep up our social life and friendship circles. My two older 'neurotypical' children needed much less input than their younger brother. But all the additional appointments made life hectic. We had no extended family nearby to give an extra hand. Choosing to make Justin's care front and centre meant my own dreams and desires took a back seat. This proved a proved a costly decision, and life began to unravel long before it started to improve. I gradually had to accept the fact that if I were to cope, we would need support in the home, so we paid for a cleaner and respite worker to mind Justin so that I could take the other children to their activities. But even with the additional help, I was struggling; there were just not enough hours in the day, let alone time for myself. At times I felt like I was drowning under the mounting workload at home and a seemingly endless stream of appointments and commitments.

I soon lost my sense of identity as my piano began to gather dust and the drinks on the deck became few and far between. Night after night, Ian and I would flop into bed exhausted. Life developed its own rhythm, but the breaks and 'me-time' that had once been within reach all but faded into the distance. I remember my mum saying how good it felt when the last of the five of us kids finally went to school, and she had a whole day to herself. The first thing she did, she told me, was head straight down to the coffee shop and just sit.

I never had that moment of relief. My work was necessary to pay the bills that kept flooding in. Fortunately, we were able to scrape together the money to pay for private therapists. This allowed Justin to have consistent therapy with a dedicated team of specialists, but it was very costly. There was no National Disability Insurance Scheme (government funding to enable participants to achieve their goals in life) in Australia in those days; it all came from our hip pocket. I quickly worked out that for me to do anything I enjoyed outside of the home, I had to perform over and above the average working housewife. All my ducks had to be lined up so that I could do what other women 'naturally' could do. I prioritised walking and going to the gym, at the expense of playing music. Somehow, I knew that my physical and mental health relied on it, and I made sure I scheduled it in my daily routine. I was always a planner, but now I began to over-plan, just to ensure that things went smoothly.

I committed to giving Justin everything he needed to progress, and I was willing to sacrifice my life and personal comforts for that to happen. They say in times of crisis, you should secure your own oxygen mask before putting on another's. It was a long while before I came to terms with this. Adrenaline and cortisol became my drugs; I lived with them pulsing through my system. They drove me when I had nothing else to give and was depleted of energy. "Unhealthy and unsustainable," the therapists chided me. "Take a break," they'd say, yet I could not shake the thought of, "Who will care as much as I do and ensure that Justin has what he needs to not just survive but thrive?"

I am sure those looking on would agree that as a family we were not thriving. In fact, we were barely making it. Like the Titanic heading for the iceberg, our circumstances seemed hopeless. If our situation had not turned and our family had not started to sail in the opposite direction, we may well have sunk.

I recall my husband and I attending a marriage counselling session where the only advice we were given was to picture life apart from each other. The therapist thought our situation was too stressful, that it simply was not sustainable to continue as we were. It was tempting to take this advice. The pressure was overwhelming and our family relationships were not healthy. My husband and I both felt relief at the thought of going our separate ways and conceding that we needed to stop trying so hard to 'make it all work'. Deep down, neither of us wanted to follow the counsellor's advice, yet we felt stuck. Caring for our son had become all-consuming. Recovering and nurturing our own relationship seemed like yet another unrealistic demand and we weren't sure we had it in us.

And so, our family continued to struggle with toxic patterns of relating and for many years, we hurt each other deeply. Having been stripped of all sense of normality, we saw only the worst in each other. It was tempting to blame the person with the most need when, really, we were all needy.

I never chose to let the music die; it simply happened. I guess I let it slip away one note at a time. A friend who is a concert flautist once said to me, "I don't know what would happen if I ever stopped playing. Would I ever play again?"

Even today, my flute sits on the top shelf of my cupboard. I cannot part with it as it reminds me of my dad, who died recently. He loved to hear me play, but the last time I played the flute was at my grandfather's funeral, many years ago. And yet, I still love to sing; it connects my spirit to God and makes me feel fully alive. Singing enabled me to come alive again, connecting me to my Father in heaven who I came to understand dearly loves me. And when my mouth could not form the words, merely listening built up my human spirit, which felt shrivelled and flat after Justin's diagnosis. My children felt the music I listened to was repetitive, but I never intended it to be; it was simply what kept me going when I was hanging in there by a thread. Worship songs became my lifeline, providing me with words of encouragement and hope. When it felt like there was no way forward, those songs spurred me to believe there would be a way.

Years after Justin was diagnosed, we moved into a larger home and I traded in my old black upright piano which desperately needed to be tuned, for an electronic Clavinova. I figured tuning was one less thing I needed to worry about. The reality was, though, that something in me shut down and my music took a backseat. In the end, I never got around to playing that instrument and even now, all these years later, it gathers dust in my living room.

Perhaps the time has come to move on. But the music is still within me . . . now it plays a different, richer tune, a melody that resounds long and loud and clear, that fights for the freedom of all who walk this path. It feels like the music retreated within me only for a season. What has emerged is a song of hope, tenacity, resilience, and healing. The girl who loved to play music is now a woman who loves to sing. Now I dance to a different beat but I sing a most glorious song. I am becoming free to be *me*. And one day, who knows, perhaps I will play my instruments once again?

Chapter Two

Dealing with Grief and Transition

At my father's funeral, the downpour of rain was so heavy that the pastor's message could barely be heard. Afterwards, a rainbow appeared, offering me assurance and a promise that Dad was in a better place, in the arms of his Heavenly Father. I was still here on earth, however, alongside a child with additional needs; where was our better place? How could I know peace in the midst of these circumstances?

After the deaths of both my grandparents and my father, I was struck by the reality that life goes on; the world does not stand still, even if it feels like it should. I was internally screaming in pain and grief, yet it was like nothing around me had changed. But for me, everything had changed. My grandparents had always been the ones I could share my heart with, and now they were gone. My dad, too, was a pillar of strength for me—and a practical help. I felt their absence in my life keenly.

The grief that came with finding out Justin was developmentally delayed also felt like a death, only my son was alive. My world felt like it had been slowed right down, and even stopped for a moment. But this did not change the fact that the need still remained to eat, dress, shower, work, pay the bills, and do mundane chores. As the music in me died, so did the hopes and dreams that any mother has for her child's life. Would Justin ever speak, walk, or play? These answers took years to find, and I never knew what to say when people asked me how he was doing—so after a while, they stopped asking.

Occasions that I had once looked forward to celebrating became painful reminders of the delays. As each birthday came and went, and another milestone had not been reached, I wanted to withdraw. At first, friends included us in everything, like they always had. Still, over time, as Justin did not connect or play with their children or vice versa, the invitations became fewer and farther between. I was becoming isolated, and strangely, I was comfortable with that, embracing self-pity as my friend while nursing my grief. It was even easy to push away other families with similar issues because I was struggling to accept that I was going to be just like them.

Despite the temptation to completely shut down, I carefully chose what and with whom I remained engaged. I went back to teaching classroom music one day per week. Another mum looked after my children when they were babies, as I had always worked at least part-time. When my first two were small, this woman and I struck up a rapport. She had a much older, disabled child and when I dropped off my kids, I always tried to connect with that girl as much as I knew how. Was I somehow being prepared even then for having a child with a disability myself? When Justin was diagnosed, this mum was willing and emotionally equipped to continue caring for and loving my son. One day a week she cared for him so that I could continue to work and maintain my teaching credentials.

During the last conversation I ever had with my father before he died, he told me, "Justin needs to have a meaningful life." I cried out inside, "I know, Dad! But how do I enable him to have the opportunities he desires? There are so many obstacles in the way of him achieving his goals."

Justin has only ever really had two life goals. Justin's first goal was to be a policeman, but he changed his plan at the age of fourteen to attending Bible college and becoming a pastor; that has not changed. Accomplishing that is easier said than done, as inclusion in the workplace and even in the church is still becoming an accepted thing for people with disabilities. We are fortunate, however, that young adults like Justin are increasingly supported in the workplace.

The Australian National Disability Insurance Scheme requires participants to state their goals at their yearly plan review so that they can provide the funds to remove the barriers to achieving those goals. When Justin was fourteen, his statement read like this:

> I live with my parents and my brother until he got married. He was in the army before then, so I did not see him very much. I also live with my sister, who is a vet nurse. I used to have an assistance dog called Gertie, but she died which made me very sad as she would help keep me calm and we would go to dog club every week and play games like flyball. I am finishing up my final year at school, where I have had strong support since I was in kindergarten. I have carers who take me out of the house for a few hours each week without Mum and Dad. Sometimes we go to the movies, play a

sport or just hang out. I would like to join a sports team one day as I love watching the NBA and cricket in particular.

I go to my church's youth group every week and I am interested in Bible studies as I would like to go to Bible college and become a pastor to help people, especially people with special needs. I have a goal to live independently so that I can live like other people. I hope to learn to make friends and develop lifestyle skills to help me achieve my dream of becoming a pastor.

This fight for Justin's 'meaningful' life is fierce, especially as I also fight to have meaning and purpose beyond the role of being a special needs mum. I have had to become an expert in problem-solving and, along the way, learn how to overcome my own struggles and baggage so that I can assist Justin with his.

A friend once said to me, "Leisa, you are not the saviour of the universe." My personality type likes to problem-solve and rise to a challenge. I knew that I had a rescuer side to me, as I always have had an inbuilt desire to help others. I am drawn to those in need and feel passionate about social justice. I resonated strongly with Prime Minister of Australia Julia Gilliard who was brought to tears while introducing legislation to help fund the National Disability Insurance Scheme. She stated with great emotion in her speech to the House of Representatives that disability was the last frontier of human rights.

With that speech, hope rose in our hearts. Finally, something was going to happen to remove the barriers that prevented people with disabilities from being able to achieve their goals. Now there was help available so that they could participate in everyday life. No longer were they to be hidden away in homes; they could venture out into society like ordinary people do every day. I felt hopeful about the additional funds we would personally receive so that as he grew, Justin could enjoy activities in the context of community. The National Disability Insurance Scheme made a big difference in being able to afford to have a support worker accompany him at times. It also provided access to transport options, enabling him to get to and from activities more independently. But a considerable time commitment was involved in ensuring that he attended and accessed everything to which he was entitled.

It still felt like life was nothing but a tight routine that consisted of work, appointments, therapy, school activities with my other children, and church. Now I became Justin's personal case manager. Overseeing his support team of often no less than fifteen people was like running a small business. I had to manage their wages and appointments, and schedule our lives around them, not to mention keeping on top of conversations about what needed to be worked on at home. The pressure mounted, and tension with other family members increased as they felt that their needs were on the backburner. One-on-one time was scarce, and the activities our children engaged in were often limited to those that fitted in with Justin's needs. Life was a juggling act, and there did not seem to be enough hours in the day to keep up with the demands.

In the early years, I resisted letting go of too much. I really did not want to lose myself in meeting the needs of my special needs child, so I clung to what I could. It was not uncommon for friends or colleagues to say things like, "You leave it; we'll do it. You have so much on your plate." At the time, this provided some relief to my overstuffed schedule. I was grateful, though in hindsight, I should not have let go of some things because doing so contributed to my isolation. Every time I let go of something I was involved in or did not step up at work, it meant that I was then passed over the next time. When other opportunities arose, people saw me as unavailable. Perhaps I was, but the reality was that those presumptions contributed to me becoming more and more disconnected in the workplace.

In the community, however, opportunities arose in addition to working part-time, I continued to oversee and run a group of community outreach playgroups four days per week. I was passionate about this. I led a small team of women, all of whom were equally keen to give back to the families of young children, and support mothers and fathers in those early years of child-raising. Justin would come to playgroup with me and slot in with the program as best he could. Soon I noticed that having Justin there encouraged other families with special needs children to attend; families of other needy children felt safe and welcome as well, though many had felt a sense of rejection in other situations due to their child's differences.

For ten years, I found a great deal of satisfaction in running those groups. Another friend began attending again with her two disabled children, and we started holiday playgroups for families with children of special needs. These groups were significant for these families because it is tough when all the programs shut down at the end of term. The stress of being home with high needs children for extended periods without any respite was enough to break any mother. So we opened up the church building, the families came for morning tea, and we provided a safe, enclosed area for the kids to let off steam before heading home for a nap.

For me, a new lifestyle was beginning to take shape. What I was doing had meaning and purpose. I was relieved that I could give back to the community I felt I was taking so much from in order to raise my child. I was grateful to be able to remain connected to families from all backgrounds. I enjoyed participating in creating a space where people could gather and be loved and accepted for who they were. This was a precious season, and I formed many friendships over that time. Our playgroups even won a community award and were recognised for their contribution to and inclusion of the community.

When Justin reached school age, Ian and I had to make a significant decision about whether he would attend a specialist school or mainstream school with support. For some families, the answer is apparent—the child's needs clearly drive the decision-making—but Justin could have gone in either direction. We felt a subtle pressure for him to participate in the specialist school. We also knew that enrolling him in a mainstream school with classroom learning support carried a risk that he might not be able to cope. However, though mainstream school would not have the same level of resources and funding, we decided to take the risk, hoping that mixing and learning in a conventional environment would enable our son to have the best chance to engage in the community.

As a little boy, Justin was fixated by trucks and cars. During recess at school, he would stand at the school fence flapping with great excitement as they drove by. The teachers would try to work out if his flapping increased when a particular colour of vehicle went by. It took a concerted effort for the teachers to get him away from the fence. It was difficult for him to even consider playing in the sandpit with other children his age.

I was thankful that Justin was spending his days with people who shared our Christian worldview and could support our family as we raised our special needs child. Looking back, I honestly believe that it was the structure of the school and the strong community that contributed to Justin's success in moving towards achieving his goal. The school structure also enabled me to maintain a balance between work, home and leisure. They say it takes a village to raise a child, and when you have a child with special needs, community is vitally important. But I knew how much work Justin was, and I struggled with feeling guilty, even though I was paying school fees to have him there. As a mother, all I wanted was what was best for my child. The predictable routines and consistent, familiar faces at school brought some normality. Still, we had many challenges and obstacles to overcome. Going to school was a milestone that made the learning delays more noticeable and we decided to have him repeat his first year at preschool. This meant he would be the oldest rather than one of the youngest in his class, but it was a wise decision which gave him a 'leg up' from the start.

Even with all three of my children now at school, I was still very busy. Ian could see how stretched I was and often asked me to accept our circumstances and let go of running the community playgroups. This was tough for me as they kept me connected to the community and other mothers, but over time, I had to recognise that my season was over. It was with great reluctance that I finally stepped back.

Close friends who cared 'a whole awful lot' gave us sound advice: "Simplify your life." They asked questions like, what one thing were we doing that made everything else easier? or what were we doing that was unnecessary? Ian and I sat down and made some hard decisions. Our hopes and dreams of a meaningful life seemed to be slipping away, but we felt a tangible sense of relief with each decision. We both stepped down from leadership positions in our church and I handed over my playgroup responsibilities and stepped off the board. We decided to move to another church where we would not feel obligated to serve to the same capacity that we had in our previous church. This church also had a much stronger youth group for our kids.

We sold some investments and upgraded our house to provide the much-needed space we required. With these changes, the add-ons were gone and our days pretty much consisted of work, appointments, after-school activities and church attendance. Was this way of functioning really what amounted to a meaningful life, I wondered, or were we just existing? Was I destined to simply go through the motions with little joy? Is this just what we needed to do so that our son could live with purpose? For many years, we wrestled with questions about what our life should really look like. Like so many parents, we were grappling with how to balance our own needs with that of our children's.

Chapter Three

The Danger of Self-Pity

Our new 'simplified' life was less hectic, and my husband, Ian, was relieved. I, on the other hand, felt consumed by yet another layer of grief. There were no more group gatherings at our home or nights out at meetings or maintenance to be done on the church building, I really missed the social interactions. It often seemed to me that when you are not serving, you are not seen; and then you are not included. The old saying 'out of sight, out of mind' seemed very appropriate. I felt too fatigued to reach out to others like I once had, and I found it interesting that as I stopped reaching out to them, they also stopped reaching out to me.

The older children missed the social interaction too. It was only years later that I realised the impact the change of church community had on my daughter; she was taken from a close-knit circle of friends and never quite made new ones in our new church. She also told me that other kids made unkind comments about Justin, as he looked and acted so differently, and she struggled with that.

Eventually we made a choice to attend an evening café-style service at our new church. The kids could run around and play while we ate a simple meal together, and during the service they could move around rather than sit still in a seat. This was a friendly service for families with additional needs and helped us transition more smoothly into the new church family.

As our community connections shrank, I fell into depression, and the situation at home became increasingly stressful. Ian and I were not connecting well; in fact, we were pulling in opposite directions. I was struggling to accept where we had found ourselves, while he found the slower pace a welcome relief. Years later, as we walked the path of transitioning Justin into adulthood, those feelings reversed. By then I was more accepting of the reality of what life would be like, while my husband was frustrated and resentful that we were not functioning like other families who had independent children.

Having additional needs in a family can strip even the most competent of parents down to the core. These added demands and challenges can last for a very long time, if not a lifetime. Regardless of age, personality or family background, the stresses are real. The financial burden associated with out-of-pocket healthcare and therapy costs, even with government support, are significant. The support coordination among the different providers— doctors, physical therapist, occupational therapist, dietician, social worker, speech therapist, psychologist, psychiatrist, podiatrist, and medical specialists like the neurologist, paediatrician, and respite providers—is extensive; the parents become responsible for keeping communication flowing between all parties. All of these responsibilities take a toll which leads to exhaustion, and the day-to-day strain of providing care is taxing on the entire family.

Justin's needs consumed a disproportionate amount of my time and greatly impacted the entire family's activities, energy, and money, leaving other individual and family needs simply unmet. We lived day by day, surviving but definitely not thriving. Each person in our family unit felt differently about our circumstances. Ian would immerse himself in leisure activities, which led to conflict in our marriage. Our two older children felt that their dreams and hopes for the future were being sacrificed. With all their parents' time and energy seeming to be invested in one person, feelings of jealously and tension arose. Justin's siblings also faced dealing with people who were unsympathetic to their brother's situation. They were particularly sensitive to the remarks or looks of others who did not know how to respond to their brother's disability. For many people with disabilities and their families this is a hurtful reality. Despite recent changes in government support and backing, there is still a long way to go for people with disabilities to be fully accepted into the community.

My daily fight for my child to be included and provided with everyday opportunities took a toll on my mental and emotional health. I began to develop a heavy demeanour, which Ian found to be quite off-putting. I was carrying a huge chip on my shoulder and had started to blame everyone else for my problems. I began to verbalize my feelings to the kind couples who had drawn alongside me, using them as a dumping ground for the injustices in my family's life. They graciously allowed me to do this for a long time, as they knew I needed to vent, but no matter how much I poured out even to safe people, the strength of my emotions did not ease. I was consumed with anger, injustice, pity, resentment, and bitterness. I felt entitled to be sorry for myself, like I deserved better. Self-pity became an automatic go-to for my situation, and over time, I became stuck in it, leading to further depression.

Self-pity is 'a self-indulgent dwelling on one's sorrows' and is actually counterproductive, as it shrinks your mindset and stops you from finding solutions to your problems. In my desperation to find solutions, the more consumed I was with my problems, the more it felt like I was in a black pit without the help of others—and even worse, without God—and I could not climb out.

In the midst of this turmoil, an older friend recommended to Ian that he attend a Christian retreat not far from our city. For whatever reason, he agreed and went away for the weekend, though I had no real clue where he was going. When he came home, however, it was clear he had been deeply affected, and recommended that I give it a go. I felt anything was worth a try, so I booked in for a weekend too. As I left, I said to Ian, "I feel like I could move to the south pole and nobody would care or ever follow me." I felt so unloved and unlovable.

I arrived at the retreat with emotional pain levels that were very high. I found it difficult to sit in the teaching sessions or to interact with people over lunch. Having become used to isolation, being in community was overwhelming. Throughout the weekend, I found myself withdrawing into the nearby bush. The fifty-four acres of bushland property had a walking track, and I wanted to disappear into the wilds and make it all go away. Whichever way I turned, life seemed unbearable. But no matter where I went that weekend, someone always found me.

On the final morning, I arose in turmoil at five a.m. and slipped out for a walk. As I sat crying under a tree, I looked up to find one of the retreat team members beside me. Sitting down on the ground, she put her arm around me. At that moment I realised that what I was running from was the very thing I craved—empathy, kindness, and love from people. I deeply longed to know that someone understood and cared about what I was going through and to have them express that to me. Remember, "Unless someone like you cares a whole awful lot, nothing is going to get better. It's not."

I left that healing retreat feeling vulnerable and scared. What was the point of all that love if I couldn't have it at home? That's when God said to me, "Leisa, all weekend you ran, and I sent people to follow you. I do notice, and wherever you are, I will never leave you nor forsake you." On that trip home, my relationship with God forever changed—I knew that amidst the pain, turmoil, grief, abandonment and loss, there was a God who cared and wanted to connect with me in my circumstances. He would not leave me or forsake me, but longed for me to draw close to Him so that He could comfort me.

Despite the insights I gained at the retreat, that one weekend did not fix my emotional state. But having begun a process of healing, I committed to attending further courses one weekend per month at the retreat centre. This was my 'me-time'. Ian had kept up his passion for night-sky photography and hobbies like gold-detecting and fishing to maintain his mental and emotional health, and he was supportive about releasing me to have a weekend away each month to process my pain. I attended a monthly retreat for many years, and now I go to offer hope to others who are struggling like I once was.

During that three-hour drive home each month, I was often raw after having allowed myself the time to process what I was really thinking and feeling inside. In the early days of my restoration journey, it was not unusual for my arrival home to go poorly. Ian may not have given me the hug I badly needed, the house might have been a mess, the kids might have been unsettled due to my absence. We sometimes fell into the trap of fighting and allowing the situation to descend into chaos. Eventually, we woke up to the fact that it was fruitless to keep on with these destructive patterns of behaviour. We made a choice to resist dumping our pain on each other.

The older couples at the retreat centre had been married for a long time, and as we got to know them, they were able to help us achieve stability and order in our family and in our marriage. They listened when we needed to download, and were only ever a phone call away. They walked with us for years, until we grew stronger and had developed better coping mechanisms. They were people who cared 'a whole awful lot'.

Attending the retreat and finding a community of people who could show me unconditional love and acceptance was key to me beginning the journey of climbing out of the hole I was in. It gave me permission to share my story, to feel compassion for myself, and to deepen my relationship with God by learning to trust in Him to help me get out of the pit. I learnt to accept that we are designed to have a range of different emotions and that what I was feeling was valid. What was not healthy was how I had been expressing or suppressing those feelings. I learned how to tell God and my safe people what I was thinking in a much healthier way. At first, it was like emptying a forty-four-gallon drum of pain one teaspoon at a time; it seemed that the intensity of my feelings would never diminish. However, as I stuck with it in prayer ministry, journaling, and counselling, those feelings started to dissipate until I felt completely different on the inside.

It was only then that I could truly become aware of my self-pity. I experienced a shift, where my gut actually started to feel healthy sadness and hurt rather than the rage and anger that I regularly dumped onto others. Now I could see that perhaps that was why some people had stayed away. By the grace of God, I began to choose not to be a victim. I stopped resisting my reality and accepted that my life is what it is; my circumstances are what they are. I learnt to embrace my lot in life. Regardless of what others thought, I determined that I could be an overcomer and have hope for my family's future. We may not look like other families or live the same way others do, but that does not mean that we cannot have a good life, a life of purpose and fulfillment.

To overcome self-pity, I first had to face my fear of rejection. For years I had lived with questions of *"what if?"* and *"why?"* I had to change the narrative to: *"What can I do to get a different outcome? How can I change my response to my situation?"* Taking responsibility for my situation enabled me to make better decisions for both myself and my special needs child. By God's grace, I started to see my situation through different lenses; I saw that my family was a blessing and that I could use my time at home to do further study and write curricula for my school. I saw that I could develop stronger managerial and leadership skills within the context of my family and that these would also benefit my workplace and ministry. I realised that I could use the time at home to express myself in a healthy way, including writing this book. I learned to be kinder to myself and prioritise some self-care.

And as I did this, the self-pity decreased and then eventually disappeared. I began to have hope for me and for my family's future. Slowly, we were beginning to climb out from under our circumstances and learning to rise above them.

Chapter Four

The Importance of Self-care

We all have stories which determine how we view ourselves and how we respond to circumstances in our lives. Our responses are as unique as each person's story. I found it really difficult to slow down and look after myself because I came from a background of high achievement and performance. I grew up in a family that was not big on displaying emotions or expressing physical affection. It seemed to me that my siblings and I received the most approval when we worked hard and achieved a good result. My mum regularly told me how much she loved me, and still does. However, my father found it difficult to express love verbally, because he had not received it in that way from his parents. It was uncommon for me as a small child to sit on Dad's lap, experience being delighted in, or hear tender words like "Daddy loves you" spoken to me.

I remember sitting around the campfire when we would go camping with other families and the other girls my age would sit in their fathers' laps while I sat beside my dad. Sometimes one of the other dads would scoop me onto his lap with his daughter and put his arm around us both. My dad found it difficult to display affection, but it did not mean that he did not love us. He just showed it in other ways, like working hard to provide for us.

Dad's family were hardworking dairy farmers, up before sunrise, milking cows seven days a week. Dad, one of eight children, did not have much time to just enjoy himself. The family was very poor, all living in a two-bedroom house, so life was about survival, running the farm to feed the family. Even though there was more money in my family than in my grandparents', my dad still worked very hard to provide for us. I am the oldest of five, so I missed out on a considerable amount of emotional nurturing, not because my father deliberately withheld it, but because it was a lack in his own life. He did not know how to express it or even realise that it was necessary. Dad saying to me in our last conversation, "Make sure that Justin has a meaningful life" was his way of expressing his love and care for Justin.

Because of this, I was not completely deprived of love, like many are, but I missed out enough to have a 'wound'; as a result, I subconsciously craved love. The lack is not necessarily the parents' fault—they can only give what has been given to them by their own parents. As I have processed this, I have come to understand why Dad was the way he was, which helped me to heal.

In earlier years, however, I was unaware of my own emotional lack and how I strived to have the love-hole in my heart filled by the approval of others. It was only during my weekends away years later that I learned that I was looking in all the wrong places to have my emotional needs met. After my son's diagnosis, I had to stop doing what I usually did to fill that void, and as a result I fell apart. My coping mechanisms of striving and performance had been taken away, and the reality of what was truly going on inside me was exposed. I felt at times like I was standing naked in front of others, whereas I usually had on a pretty good mask which had served to hide my pain for years. The real me was finally at the surface, and it was painful but, in a strange way, really good. I was no longer in control and could stop trying to be the one that spun all the plates. Instead, I learnt to trust in God to help me heal and recover to become a much healthier *me*.

As my monthly retreats unfolded, I began to discover that I was not very good at resting or taking time out for myself. In fact, I actually did not know how to rest, and that was why I was finding it so hard to step back. This was coupled with the fact that our family being home together was not very peaceful. Now that I was aware of the hole in my heart that I had been filling with my striving and performance, I went on a deeper journey of discovering me, not only for myself, but as a child of God.

My faith in God became essential as I began to truly understand that I was loved, not for what I do but for who I am. The fact that people had stepped back from me no longer hurt so much, as I realised God would never step back from me. This was all part of my restoration process. It was like I was literally being sanded back to bare boards and then refurbished, all shiny and new.

I started making changes to my weekly routine that allowed time out for me. Instead of feeling cross if Ian was fishing again, I began to think "I can do that too." So, we started to negotiate our leisure times so that we could both have a break. I love swimming, and for many years it worked out that when the kids went to bed early I could go to the pool in the evening. I took every opportunity I could to walk, and it was a bonus that my oldest child loved walking with me. In fact, it was one day while we were we out walking that we found our second home. Seeing an 'open home inspection', we walked in to take a peek. Two weeks later, we had exchanged contracts, and it was ours!

Most significantly, I discovered during this season the importance of creativity, and how, where there is deep emotional pain, creativity brings healing and wholeness. Before, my life had predominantly been lived out of my head. I found it difficult to relax and just go with the flow. I first discovered this when I went to university and ended up hanging out with the jazz department. I was a classical musician, and it was the notes on the page, which were predictable and set, that kept me in my security bubble, safe and in control even when playing music. At university, a bunch of guys invited me to jam with them, and I literally froze! I could not just jam with only five notes written on a page. Yet during that time, they helped to unlock my inner musician; I became more relaxed and started to let the music flow through me, though I was definitely a work in progress. Years later, when I took a job as a music teacher, my teaching partner—would you believe it—was a jazz musician. He knocked a bit more of the uprightness out of my playing, and I would practice jamming with jazz in my classes with five-to-ten-year-old children. They wouldn't care if I made a mistake, right?! We all made mistakes and improvised together, and it was so much fun!

By now, I had well and truly let the music die. However, a new side to my creativity was about to emerge. I was never one to enjoy crafting or painting; I left it to my sister and mother, who are both very good at it. So, when painting classes and creativity weekends were offered at the retreat centre I attended, I immediately thought it was not for me.

Over time, however, I came to discover firsthand that creativity is an essential part of self-care and inner healing. Creativity links us together holistically — spirit, soul, and body. We are not just a mind or a body or a spirit; we are all three. And if you are a Christian, then your spirit is connected to God's Spirit in a deep and personal way. So, creativity is an added dimension for me personally, and perhaps the crux of why I have found self-care through creativity so beneficial.

It is through creativity that I learnt to think differently. Creativity bypasses my mind and links me to my spirit and the Holy Spirit. It became a way of me letting go and letting God into parts of my life that I had resisted dealing with. As old patterns and habits of thinking were unblocked, I could see what lay behind my thought processes. This in turn enabled me to express my grief and pain more easily by taking it to my Heavenly Father.

When we are in difficult circumstances, it is easy to disengage from life. As my story unfolded, that was happening to me. In a way, it was like I had become powerless. I had to learn new ways to do things and even how to respond to situations. I had to become creative in my problem-solving while allowing God, through creativity, to show me what needed to be changed or rewired, so that I could move through hopelessness and despair to a life of hope and freedom.

Creativity helped me own and take responsibility for my story. For example, I discovered that the reason I didn't want to do a painting class was because I believed that my painting would not be good enough. Whenever I had tried to paint as a child, my mother — being much better at it — had always lovingly corrected me. So, I stopped painting and focused on music instead. Music was my thing, and art was theirs. I felt incredibly vulnerable going into my first painting class, but part of my healing was to be brave enough to face my vulnerabilities. My first painting turned out better than I expected; it was no Picasso, but it was mine, and I was happy with that.

Part of self-care is allowing yourself time to heal. It may be painting, drawing, knitting, quilting, writing, playing an instrument, song writing, designing cards—but whatever it is, creativity is at its root. I even had a crack at writing poetry. I found a space where I could be real and allow healing to come as God connected me through creativity to difficult feelings and experiences. It was where I could explore hard emotions, deal with the pain I was feeling and heal from the hurt I had caused others in my brokenness.

One day a friend felt prompted to bring all of her scrapbooking material over to my place to teach me how to scrapbook. As I pulled pictures from photo albums, I was able to connect my memories with my emotions and celebrate the good times we had had in our family and be grateful for what we did have. This was the beginning of a scrapbooking journey lasting several years, as we shared life through our photos and talked about our struggles, hopes and dreams. This was all a part of my self-care, giving myself permission to create and do something that I was very much beginning to enjoy, as well as sharing in the added bonus of friendship. Our scrapbooking had no other purpose than relaxing with a friend and being creative.

I have also kept in touch with the carers' groups in my region and found this to be a valuable source of support. Most of these groups coordinate and run activities that nurture and build up one's spirit. They often also offer counselling and mental health support for carers at reasonable rates. For many years, our family was involved with a young carers group in which my two older children attended activities especially for the siblings of children with a disability. It enabled them to build relationships with likeminded friends who could understand their situation. They also had opportunities to attend movies, camps, ice skating, waterslides, bowling, zoo trips and much more at a low cost for special needs families.

As I began to appreciate our life, I battled intense feelings of guilt that life was suddenly about us and our need to do enjoyable things, rather than serving in the community with every spare minute. I had to give myself permission to receive. I had built a life on giving, and it was not easy to be the one on the receiving end. This was particularly true when I would occasionally get comments like, "There are a lot of perks with having a disabled child." And perhaps there are, if you want to look at it that way. For example, in all of the twenty-plus years my brother has lived overseas, we were never able to visit him. One day, we decided to make the trip, which we've never regretted, and he took us to Disneyland, where special needs families get a fast pass to the front of the queue. That day, I think we were all grateful for Justin's disability as we got to go on so many rides and had front seats in all the shows. The self-care we experienced at Disneyland, if only for that moment, is something for which we will be forever grateful. Having the "J-Pass," as my brother called it, gave us an amazing day of family fun. On another occasion, Justin was given front row seats at the test cricket in London, United Kingdom. All the tickets had sold out, but an extremely kind lady found a space for him front and centre.

As the years have passed, I have realised that these sorts of moments are so essential, both individually and as a family. It may not need to be as lavish as going to Disneyland, but finding holiday accommodation that suits special needs families is very important, because what is relaxing for every other family can literally be a nightmare for a family with additional needs. The pressure and worry that families go through under so many difficult circumstances leaves me speechless, and I salute all those mums and dads for hanging in there. It is not easy.

I had a pivotal moment sitting at my desk at work one day. As a teacher and coordinator of a department, I have a lot of course writing to do and even study to keep upskilled. Therefore, for years, all my time off work had been taken up with either writing courses or studying. I was verging on burnout, and one day it all came crashing over me when a colleague bragged about how relaxing the holidays were. I thought "I just cannot get a break!" That evening I went home and said to Ian, "No matter the cost, I want a real holiday." I insisted it be a cruise so that I would not have to lift a finger, and everything would be done for me. That kicked off a small season of travel for us, which is something many families do all the time, but we had felt was inaccessible to us because of Justin's needs. We had learned how to make it work and navigate all the ups and downs and had readjusted our expectations. Learning that we could travel and not just be stuck at home made a big difference to our family's mental health.

As a result of our discovery, Ian and I feel passionate about offering holidays for the disabled. Together, we built a specially certified unit under our house so that people who might not otherwise consider having a holiday due to the challenges of travelling with special needs children, can enjoy visiting our hometown.

The truth is, self-care does matter. We are not machines. We are living, breathing human beings who need to learn to take care of ourselves. It is not selfish or unreasonable to expect to have time out for yourself and your family, just like other families do. Yet somehow, when there are additional needs in a family, it can feel impossible to get away or that it just takes too much effort. I assure you that taking time for self-care is worth fighting for. It is worth investing in yourself, in putting on your own oxygen mask so that you can then give aid to your loved ones.

Chapter Five

Combatting Stress

My husband sometimes remarks, "Leisa, you are so uptight. Can you just relax?" Ian really struggles with the fact that I do not seem to have an off-button. My friend once said, "You are always thinking." That is what it is like living in my brain, and I still have to fight it all the time. To 'let go and let God,' as they say, I had to learn that I do not have to be the problem-solver of every situation, even if it feels like I do.

A big part of my self-care has always been to exercise. When I was struggling with depression many years ago, my general practitioner recommended that I swim if I wanted to avoid antidepressants. I took his advice, and to this day swimming is my favourite exercise for many reasons. Swimming engages the total body, and it is a great aerobic exercise. The extra blood and oxygen help you become more alert and focused. It releases endorphins, the feel-good hormones, in the body; it literally lights up our brains! This is the opposite of cortisol, the stress hormone, which can wear down the brain's ability to function correctly.

If you are a caregiver, it is vital to lower your levels of cortisol. I have to be honest here, that I am writing this chapter to myself as much as to you. I am absolutely convinced of the need to lower cortisol, and I am a work in progress. Swimming was what kept me sane and off antidepressants. Finding the time can be an issue, and in this season, it is simply not practical for me to drive to the pool, get changed, swim laps, shower, dry my hair and drive home again.

A local women's gym has been the best fit for my current lifestyle, as it offers a thirty-minute workout that I can complete just three times per week. I fit this in between work and home. The gym also has monthly weigh-ins and measures, which I appreciate because I have struggled to keep within my weight range as I have gotten older. Many factors, which I am figuring out, contribute to this. Special needs mothers often have higher levels of cortisol when compared to mothers of children without disabilities, although interestingly this is not always the case—sometimes special needs mothers even have lower cortisol levels, having become desensitized to stress. In fact, researchers at the University of Wisconsin found that, in the same way soldiers in combat zones become desensitized to danger and therefore have reduced cortisol levels, mothers of autistic children had significantly lowered cortisol levels than normal. Repeated exposure to stress is known to cause diminished stress hormones over time. If you are in this situation, you have to be very careful because the lower levels of cortisol can mask caregiver burnout.

I have struggled with fatigue for many years and find it challenging to know the exact source. I have prioritized keeping up with health checks, and I ask my general practitioner for a full screen every year. Caregivers often avoid going to the doctor themselves because they do not want to leave their loved one even for a short time, or they prioritize their loved one's appointments over their own. It is vital to have a back-up caregiver for situations like this.

I have also found it difficult to be completely honest with health care providers about the causes of stress I am experiencing. It is embarrassing to admit that you are not coping. I saw myself as a competent person, and yet there were many days when my autistic son had meltdowns and I just did not know what to do except call out, "Help me, God!"

Our family all struggled with our health and often wondered who could truly understand what we were going through. We have learned to be proactive rather than reactive with both emotional and physical health, in order to nip problems in the bud, especially when it comes to health issues related to a stressful family life. Making the choice to treat these issues means that we have been able to better manage caregiver burnout. Ian and I have learned to identify burnout before it gains a foothold, and take steps to alleviate it. We do this by negotiating time away individually. For Ian, it may be a photography trip to his favourite lake, while I might choose a couple of nights of mother-daughter time at a health retreat with a lap pool. These separate trips were an adjustment for me. When we married, I assumed that our holidays would mostly be together. But given our circumstances, to make a break possible, this is how we manage. I am still coming to terms with it, as my natural desire is to holiday together. Our reality is not what my idea of marriage was. I have had to work through this adjustment in my way of thinking.

Adrenaline is also an enemy, as my mind is always on alert. I feel a constant need to think about what needs to be sorted in my son's life and how to best care for our family's needs. I have also become aware that my role advocating for my son causes me to overproduce adrenaline. When you have a child with high demands, you become that child's voice. "Unless someone like you cares a whole awful lot, nothing is going to get better. It's not." I am that person for Justin.

I realise now that right from the get-go, I felt like I had my boxing gloves on. It started with the words from the paediatrician, "He will only have the mind of a fifteen-month-old," and "He won't speak." I immediately rejected those words. My body was always in fight mode, even when kind people were trying their best to help us. I stood against the diagnosis and prayed fervently; I refused to let that be Justin's reality. I followed every piece of advice for therapy. Because I threw myself so entirely into managing his therapy appointments, I was continually anxious, stressed and full of adrenaline.

Ultimately, I was told that we had to label Justin to get the best help for him, or there would be no funding. I reluctantly agreed, as I knew deep down that there was a God-given purpose and plan for his life that would unfold in time, but I was distressed to read statements in his reports that said most developmental milestones were delayed. I felt that I was under a real attack where, rather than people being for us, they were against us. In hindsight, I think this was part of the grieving process and another indication of how hard I was finding to not accept the diagnosis.

I started to reject people before they could leave me. I did not want to be pitied, and sometimes I felt offers of help were token and not what we really needed. I did not understand in the beginning just how important even the smallest amount of support was, and that Justin's team and I were in for a long journey together. It was not a matter of attending six speech therapy sessions and being done; instead, we'd be working with the same therapist from the time Justin was three until he was fourteen. If the therapist set boundaries on how much time we had for therapy, it was because we were chipping away at a vast mountain. I initially just wanted Justin to progress immediately and quickly so that I could get on with living.

The reality was that by resisting the process, I was delaying my healing and Justin's recovery. My body was producing a deadly cocktail of cortisol and adrenaline, mixed with negative emotions such as rage, resentment, bitterness, fear, doubt, and rejection—all of which damage one's health. Becoming aware of my inner health and external responses was necessary so that I could address them.

As well as attending the retreat courses each month, I started seeing a physiotherapist regularly to help me release the tension in my body. I discovered that I was carrying significant amounts of stress in my jaw and face and would clench my teeth at night. "Relax, relax," he would say, but I had no idea how to do that. He gave me many exercises to perform, and I eventually added a regular stretching routine that helped to iron out the day's tension and bring a physical release.

Still, at many points, I honestly felt I had to put the boxing gloves back on. It seemed that no matter how hard I tried, I was always fighting to be in the moment and let things roll. It also seemed that each time I took my finger off the pulse, things fell apart or were missed. In all fairness, the mistakes were not intentional. Still, when people (even therapists) do not understand special needs, things do get overlooked. While this may not be such a big deal for a normal person, those missing elements can be enormous for a person with special needs.

Many times I would discover that support providers had forgotten to let us know the respite worker could not come, or the person would not turn up or turned up to the wrong venue. I would be at work feeling stressed because the team I was relying on had let us down yet again. Or, there would be a camp or excursion where no one fully understood Justin's needs, and therefore did not adequately provide for them. They just assumed he would be fine or would manage. The good news is that things are changing within schools in Australia; now, students with special needs are required to have individual learning plans. There is increased pressure to ensure that they are included in schools fully, just like any other student.

Health issues like the ones I have been fighting to keep in check are important because they can so quickly get out of control. Caregivers spend so much time meeting the needs of their loved one that they either honestly forget or simply do not have time to care about themselves—especially when it comes to adding additional appointments into the weekly schedule when already balancing a child's appointments. When Justin was older, I utilized respite workers to take him to and from the appointments, and it has been a lifesaver when they are dependable. It has helped to alleviate a lot of stress.

Currently, I am struggling with health and stress levels again as we transition Justin into adulthood. It has not been a smooth transition. For more than two years now, I have engaged in countless conversations with numerous stakeholders about what Justin's future pathway could look like. It may seem like no big deal, as it is something that countless young people undertake each year. Granted, this year was like no other due to the effects of Covid-19, and youth hopelessness is, in my opinion, becoming an epidemic. But for my son, he has a goal; he knows where he wants to go and what he wants to do. Yet the stress involved in enrolling him in a humble 'certificate course' has been monumental.

I do not believe that employers, education providers, or even therapists fully understand the stress and impact of navigating such a transition. Before each conversation, I have to breathe deeply and trust that my God has it all in hand. I just cannot separate this journey from my faith; without God on my side, I have no clue how I would survive, let alone thrive. Ultimately, it is finding the time and space to rest in Him that enables me to diffuse the stress levels. I am getting better at this, but still find it challenging. A friend said, "Just keep asking God what is next." So, that is what I do, as I can't solve these problems on my own.

Constant banging on closed doors and being told 'no' takes a toll on your health. It seems I am always going against the tide, and it is hard; I long for the journey to be easy. Deep within though, each time a battle is won for Justin or for me personally, I am convinced that it is being won on behalf of many families. The question is, should I stop fighting, especially when there are health implications? For me, it is a delicate balance as I know that I am not to do this in my own strength but to trust that if God is for me, who can be against me?!

Still, I have been given a body to take care of, and I am the only one who can do that. I need to take time to rest, reflect on life and connect with God. Scheduling in quiet times and breaks every day is essential if we are to keep cortisol and adrenaline under control. Some seasons are more challenging to navigate than others. Still, as long as I have that goal in mind, I can bring myself back onto the right path—a path that resists overwork, striving and performance, which produces these deadly toxins in my body.

I love having deep and rich conversations with people, and I had one today. Someone asked me whether it is more stressful to have choices or to live with no options and just be in the moment. People with lifelong disabilities live a life of little, if any, choice. They do not have access to the everyday opportunities that others have, and often rely on others to decide for them or with them. When people lose the ability, or are born with little or no ability to make choices over their own lives, it puts a strain on them mentally, emotionally, and physically. Our bodies are made to be healthy. Yet, circumstances can thrust people into situations which mean the body is fighting on every level. It is important to be aware of the impact on ourselves as caregivers and also on those with special needs, for their health is just as likely to be negatively affected as ours is.

I am grateful that no matter how difficult our circumstances, we can learn valuable skills to become and remain healthy. For me, I can only honestly do this in Christ, as He is the one that offers me the rest and peace that strengthens and sustains me.

Chapter Six

THE BENEFITS OF PETS

The end of each school day was always an interesting time when the children were younger. Tired and sometimes cranky from a long day at school, all three kids were always keen to get into the house, have afternoon tea and plop in front of a favourite television show. It was no contest, but for whatever reason, Justin decided to make it one. The car would hit the driveway, and there would be a mad dash to the doorway; he had to be first into the house. This was unacceptable to our second child, and the race was on; it could get quite ugly if he did not win. I was exhausted before I even got in the door.

It was a welcome relief when what had become a daily ritual was broken up by a small black bundle huddled on the door mat. Our daughter, who loves animals, was immediately distracted and scooped the small black dog into her arms. Without hesitation, the critter was in the house. It turned out that he belonged to our neighbours, an escapee from their back yard. Over the coming weeks and months, however, Rebel became a regular visitor. Our daughter especially loved that stocky little black dog who had a mind of his own, and his presence made for much happier arrivals home.

Rebel would trot around the neighbourhood like he owned the place, and it was not uncommon to come driving through the underpass to see him scampering along on the side of the road. I would pull over, and the kids would pick him up and bring him back home; he certainly didn't like to be contained. In fact, he started spending more time at our place than his own. One day our neighbour came over and said, "Any time your daughter wants to get Rebel for a play, she can open our side gate and get him." Of course, she absolutely wanted to do that, and each afternoon would slip next door to find her best friend to hang out with.

Sadly, we learned out neighbours were leaving. By that time, we had all become quite fond of Rebel, who had snuck his way into our hearts. Then, mere days before their moving date, we were out in the front garden when our neighbour approached Ian. "Listen, um . . . I am downsizing, and there is no room in my place for Rebel. Would you like to have him?" Wow! This was quite an offer. Neither of us had owned a dog before, but we could see the benefits to our family, especially our second child. Rebel provided a buffer between her and her special needs brother. He was company and comfort and a heap of fun. So, without thinking it through too much, we both said yes!

To make things even more special, Rebel's arrival in our family coincided with our daughter's birthday, so he was an unexpected but very well received gift. Rebel was seven years old when we adopted him into our family. I really had no clue about taking on a dog. How hard could it be? I assumed we'd need to feed him twice a day, walk him, and clean up his poos in the backyard. Of course, there were the usual promises of "Don't worry, Mum and Dad, I will look after him." But we soon realised there was quite a bit of responsibility in becoming a dog owner.

We muddled along and tried our best to keep him safe and in our back yard, but we must have been struggling, as we had a visit from our neighbour across the road. She was a kind lady who loves dogs and, like many in our street, was very fond of Rebel as he regularly dropped in to visit. She looked a little sheepish, but finally it came out. "I hope you will not be offended," she said, "but how would you feel if I sponsored Rebel? Like paid for his food and vet care?" This was unexpected. I wondered if we were not taking good enough care of him. I was a little taken aback, but when I thought about it, I realised that perhaps it would ease the burden a little as finances were quite tight. So, we agreed. It turned out to be a very good decision because with her support came a wealth of knowledge about caring for and raising dogs. She was just so attentive to their needs and could pick up when Rebel was unwell and determine what care he needed.

I came to realise that even though I thought I loved animals, I did not really know how to connect with them. I did not realise how sensitive and engaging they really are and the incredible role they can play in a family, especially one with additional needs. Somehow, Rebel was a stabiliser in what was a tumultuous and crazy time in our family. He was an outlet for all of the children as he would snuggle with them, fetch a ball, and just be jolly difficult to catch. They loved to take him for walks, which he loved. In fact, we could see the benefits of having Rebel in our family so much that I put in an application for an assistance dog for Justin, but also for our daughter, since she loved animals so much. Rebel was also getting on in years, and we were all so attached that we could not imagine life without our stocky old dog.

It was with great excitement sometime later that we received an email letting us know that an application we had submitted to an organisation called 'Assistance Dogs Australia' had been approved. I cannot speak highly enough of the people in this wonderful organisation who match families with therapy dogs; I'm so grateful for the role they play in any family that has special needs. I have a different perspective now when I see therapy dogs come into the hospital wards and nursing homes, as I know firsthand how much they can brighten someone's day. *Assistance dogs* are working animals that are specially trained to help people who live with physical and mental disabilities (including autism) to move around, engage in everyday activities and tasks, and be more independent. Our therapy dog was essentially a failed guide dog, but the moment we laid eyes on Gertie, we all fell in love.

It was her exuberance, wide cheeky grin and absolute joy that immediately won our hearts. When she arrived, she burst through our front door and did laps around the back yard. When she jumped exuberantly into our fishponds, we knew it was the fish that would have to go. Her arrival was one of the happiest days in our family's life, and she was a healing balm to our somewhat ravaged souls. We simply loved her.

For our family, there were many benefits to having a therapy dog. She taught empathy and appropriate interpersonal skills and helped the kids develop social skills. Gertie was also a soothing presence, as she was tuned in to pick up on anxiety and stress and bring calm. This helped Justin learn to pick up on the social cues that are imperative to human relationships.

She also drew us into society. We joined the local dog club, and this became a wonderful point of connection for Justin. I discovered that with Gertie at his side, people would talk with him, and when they asked him questions, he felt confident to answer them. He even won the award for Junior Dog Handler of the Year!

Extensive training had been invested into Gertie, and she was very responsive to commands and attentive to the children's needs. She bonded to them and would draw alongside them whenever they were anxious or stressed. She literally became their best friend. The added responsibility of her care was good for Justin, as he had to look outside of his autistic world and think of Gertie's needs — and she certainly let him know that she had them. She loved food, and we learnt very quickly not to leave anything lying around. In the early days of her living with us, we lost a lamb roast as well as two kilograms of expensive lamb diced for a favourite curry, loaves of bread, and freshly baked muffins; there was nothing she would not consume, and she had no filter warning her when to stop. Yes, she was a Labrador!

Gertie came on many adventures with us. Because she was an assistance dog, we were able to take her on family holidays. She loved water, especially the beach, where she would run crashing into the waves. We even took her on a flight across Australia to visit my sister and her family, and she had a wonderful time. Being able to travel with Gertie eased the stress and anxiety Justin felt when he was in a new place, as his travelling companion was there to soothe and comfort him. By focussing on her needs, making sure that she was safe and fed, Justin was able to adjust better to foreign environments. The additional work of taking Gertie was well worth it, as it meant that our holidays went a little more smoothly.

With the arrival of Rebel and then our therapy dog, our home became a lot happier; the dogs had a way of taking our attention off of ourselves and making us laugh, whether it was their antics when chasing each other through the house, chasing their own tails or climbing all over us as we tried to watch television together. It was a crazy madhouse, but also a heap of fun with them in our lives. I would wake up each morning to Gertie galloping down the hall to put her face right beside mine in bed and give me a welcoming lick and grin. She gave me emotional input, pouring in love and affection; in her own doggy way she made up for some of the lack in my life from which I had been healing.

I truly believe that animals, especially dogs, can play a significant role in the healing process. Reaching out to your local assistance dog organisation can be a positive start to discovering what is possible for you and your family. The role of therapy dogs is to react and respond to people and their environment under the guidance and direction of their owner. For example, an individual might be encouraged to gently pat or talk to a dog to teach them 'sensitive touch' and help them express their thoughts.

And the benefits have been shown to work both for both people and animals. Research shows that in response to the human-animal bond, dogs produce oxytocin (a hormone that increases trust in humans) and have decreased cortisol levels when connecting with their owner.

Rebel was fourteen when he died. One day, he just stopped eating, and we discovered he had a tumour. The veterinarian operated on him, but found that the tumour was too far advanced, and so we made the painful decision to not wake him up. We buried Rebel under a grass tree in our back yard. Everyone grieved, but Gertie more than any of us. She missed her playmate terribly. Her happy-go-lucky personality disappeared and she began moping around the house. The kids noticed it, of course, and started pleading with us for another dog.

That is how Furzy, a Lagotto Romagnolo X Cattle Dog, came into our lives. We had never heard of this Italian water dog breed before, but we found him as an eleven-week-old puppy at the local RSPCA shelter. Furzy was a dynamo right from the start. With a mind of his own, he fitted right in with our kids—it seemed he didn't like to be told what to do either!

The 'little boy,' as Ian called him, bonded very closely with him, and they are best mates still today. Gertie and Furzy were also firm friends and stayed that way until Gertie's death four years later. Sadly, at the age of eight, she too developed cancer. Though she survived the surgery, she had an accident post-surgery which tragically took her life. We had a week filled with hope only to be taken down to the pit of deep and heavy grief. Not one of us was unaffected; in fact, we were shell-shocked, wondering how we would ever recover. She was the one who had brought joy and laughter into our lives and enabled us to bond as a family.

Gertie taught me a lot in the time we had her. Prior to Rebel coming into our family, I would not have seen myself as a 'dog person', especially allowing them to come into the house or lick me in the morning as I woke up! But Gertie taught me how to receive the same unconditional love and affection she gave us all. She showed me how critical it is to bond well in relationships and to both give and take. She gave as much as she took, and I saw my son's emotional and social skills grow and develop as he learned to interact with her and care for her needs.

Our friends at the Assistance Dogs association were saddened to hear the news and kindly sent a card. We were hurting so badly and even the thought of replacing her was too much to cope with. Furzy was lonely and stricken with grief too. Justin wanted an assistance dog, but we realised it might not be the right timing. Eventually, it was our second child who found and bought her own puppy, Peggy, who we all love and adore. I call her my granddaughter, as I know that one day, she will leave home with her owner and I will have to be satisfied with visits.

I realise now that the decision we made all those years ago for the sake of the kids became the greatest source of joy and healing. I never expected to bond so closely with any, much less all, of the pets that have come into our lives in recent years. Their presence has kept me in the moment, made me laugh and provided me with much-needed distractions at times. Ian and I are both so glad that we got over ourselves and opened up our hearts and lives to the wonderful world of having pets.

Since having dogs, I have weakened and said yes to a rescue cat called Mario. Who would have thought that I could be so flexible, especially when they trapse mud from the yard through my house?! Justin hopes to have another assistance dog and a cat in the future. He discovered a love of cats when Mario came into our lives. All I know is that one day when Ian and I are empty nesters, I am already planning to purchase my own dog. I love taking long walks over the mountain trails near our house, and having a doggy companion alongside is a treat, especially as they also motivate me to keep fit!

Our beloved Gertie will be forever in our hearts and remembered for the healing and hope that she brought into our family during a very challenging season. She is planted under a willow tree with the loveliest yellow paper daisies all around her. We also planted a wattle grove in her memory as her golden yellow coat lit up any room.

As I end this chapter, I want to honour all those who raise therapy and service dogs. Thank you for the hours you invest in their training so that families like ours can receive the blessings and joys of having them become part of our lives. Many organisations train dogs, and I encourage my readers to learn about them and see what support they can offer you. Receiving a well-trained, housebroken dog is so helpful when you have so much already on your plate as a special needs family. The experience vastly exceeded our expectations, and I am so grateful for all that we gained as a family from our time with Gertie and the support from Assistance Dogs Australia.

I chose to end Part One of this book with this section on pets because they have been such a significant part of our story—and my personal story. Our pets have bridged the gap of pain and confusion when we have not known what to do with ourselves or where to go. They have provided light relief, much-needed laughter, stress reduction (though they may also have created a bit of stress—like running through a muddy back yard then jumping all over my bed); but most important of all, they have been instrumental in enabling our family to heal.

PART 2

MOVING FORWARD

Chapter Seven

Getting from Here to There

Over the years I have read many self-help books which have assisted me to move from 'here' to 'there'. Because of this, I felt compelled to write one based on my own experiences. But the book that has been most helpful to me personally in enabling me to move forward in spite of my circumstances, is God's Word, the Bible. It contains everything needed to have a fulfilling and meaningful life. For that reason, I want to weave some perspectives from the Bible into this section.

The first step in terms of getting from here to there, is to locate where you are now. Stop for a minute and ask yourself the question: *What does my life look like on the date that I am reading this book?* The reality is that no one has ever fully 'arrived'. We can always find some area in our lives where we can grow and develop to become all that we are created to be.

Take a moment to write down or reflect on what your life currently looks like, and then consider how you would like it to look in the near future, the more distant future and well into the future. You may find it difficult to write a list of positives. Start with what you have, no matter how small, and see whether your list grows over the next few days. We sometimes are so focused on the negative that we fail to see the good in our daily lives right away. Begin by writing down ten things that you like about your life. Let me share a few examples from my own life:

WHERE I AM *(HERE)*

I have:

- a job.
- friends I can talk to when I need to unload and receive emotional support.
- a supportive community.
- stronger, closer family relationships than I used to have.
- a place to live and have been able to renovate the house to make it disability-friendly.
- loving pets who are a bright spark in my day.
- places to go for walks just outside my front door.
- a husband who is becoming more aware of the pressures in my life.
- increased awareness of what I need to do to look after my health.
- children that I enjoy relationships with as they move into adulthood.

Now write down ten things that you would like to improve or change about where you are now in relation to where you would like to be.

Here are some of mine:

WHERE I WANT TO BE *(THERE)*

I would like to:

- have time to include swimming in my weekly routine.
- have a deeper, more understanding relationship with my husband, and time to invest in 'us' each week.
- have more flexibility to manage my son's needs as they arise.
- see Justin living independently with supports so he can achieve his life goals.
- be able to afford independent accommodation for Justin in a safe community.
- establish my own business.
- increase my social life and do more fun activities.
- have my own dog, probably a retriever.
- grow closer to God and deal with the fears that are holding me back.
- have a much lighter, happier personality.

Getting where you want to be usually does not happen all at once. I remember when I set out on what I call my 'healing journey', the course director would say to us, "What you are about to embark on is a ten-year process." *Ten years!* I screamed in my head. I felt like giving up immediately, but I did not! I had to accept it was okay, due to the complexity of the needs in our family, to be a tortoise and not a hare in this stage of my life. Please note this may not be the case for you. One situation may move faster than another, but the most important thing is that you start moving forward without worrying about how long it may take to get to your 'there'.

I knew where I longed to be, but how to get there was unclear. I longed to be emotionally stronger so that I could not only cope better with my family circumstances but also become a person who was living well in this world and able to help and support other people.

It was as if I could not see the forest for the trees. Those ten years have well and truly passed now, and I can confidently say that I am not the same person who first walked into that retreat course. I began fearful, self-absorbed, angry, and full of self-pity. I was even told at one point (in what turned out to be an honest and loving conversation) that my heart was cold. I had become numb to the needs of others because I had allowed my own pain to overwhelm and drive much of my life.

The sample lists that I shared are completely different to the ones I would have written ten years or so ago. Ten years later, I am becoming a woman who is more trusting, less fearful and able to walk amid adversity knowing that, in spite of difficulties, there is a God who loves and cares for me, and has my back no matter what. I cannot personally separate my journey from my faith, because God is the key to my healing.

Back then, my 'here' was fear-based. I was driven by the 'what ifs' which led to *if onlys* which led to great discouragement. I tended to look at what had happened and allow self-pity to take over. When I tried to look ahead, I could not see a way forward. My husband struggled with this even more than I did, often describing our situation as intractable, terminal and hopeless. This is not helpful language. Perhaps it didn't help that we are such opposites—me with the glass half-full view, and him seeing the glass half-empty—that made me dig in my heels and search for the pathway out of our mess.

One of the people who cared 'a whole awful lot' compared our situation to a chariot that is stuck in a deep rut. At first, the wheels are barely able to turn, but as the chariot driver perseveres, they start to move, and slowly but surely the chariot begins edging along the ruts. The wheels are slow to gain momentum, but eventually they turn freely and the chariot can be driven out of the rut and down the road.

This is exactly how I would describe the journey out of the mess and chaos of our disordered family life. At first it seemed like nothing would ever change, possibly even that we were wasting our time. But though our progress was small at first, all change was good change because it kept edging us forward. As time went on, however, all those changes that had seemed so insignificant or like they made hardly any difference, began to add up to a big shift overall.

That meant we became a family who started to work together as a team, could relate to each other with less stress and tension, and had each other's backs. For us, getting 'there' meant being able to relate better to one another and work together instead of pulling against each other in frustration. We also learned to support one another and give each other space to process our different needs and responses.

Notice that I am not painting a perfect picture of our 'here' or our 'there'. That is unrealistic. Like everyone, we are a work in progress, but we are so much better than we were when we set out. Also, it is important to acknowledge that the deeper the rut or the bigger the mess, the bigger and longer the effort to get out. The progress may seem very slow, but you will get there, whatever your 'there' is. This is why it is so important to identify where you are now and where you would like to be.

KEYS TO GETTING FROM 'HERE' TO 'THERE'

Change your perspective

For our family, we needed to change how we looked at our situation. One of the stresses we struggled to bring into order was our tendency to live in denial. The reality is that we do have a child with special needs, our life is impacted, and his needs may or may not change. We wanted to keep living the way we had always lived. But when I started to accept my situation for what it was and stopped resisting, it was much easier to move forward in my own healing and relate to my family in a much healthier way. I started to accept that my life was on a different path from what I had expected, and I had to change my perspective about what constituted the right or wrong way to live. In fact, I had to accept that there is not a one-size-fits-all approach to life, that our family did not 'fit the mould', and that shades of grey can be okay.

My perspective of what a Christian family looked like also had to change. I had to come to terms with the fact that it was okay to go to church without having it all together. This challenged me from a faith perspective, and I had to really search the Bible to see how it applied to families with special needs. It felt like we did not fit at all, as no matter how hard we tried, we were not even on the outside—much less the inside—in terms of being accepted at church. The reality is that I was trapped in a pattern of looking for approval in all the wrong places.

The even more important reality is that I was already approved of by my Heavenly Father. So, I did not need to turn up to church with it all together. I needed to understand that God loves and accepts us right where we are. I had to change how I viewed God—

realising that He was not a harsh Father looking down on me and my situation in judgement, but a loving Father who longs for the best in me and wants me to come to Him with all of my problems.

When I changed my view of God, it enabled me to change my perspective on how I viewed my life. I do not need to look to others for their stamp of approval or for affirmation about whether I am doing things right or wrong. I believe in accountability, but only from those who have a more complete understanding of my situation. I needed to learn to listen to those who could speak into my life with discernment and have the wisdom to correct me when I was genuinely going off-track with an imbalanced perspective. What I found interesting is that, after about ten years, very little about my external circumstances had changed, but because my internal outlook had changed, I was able to cope with my external circumstances.

Know that your feelings are valid

It is important to acknowledge what you really think and feel about your circumstances. I used to feel guilty for being so angry and full of self-pity. Yet I still felt that life is not fair. I believed I had been robbed of my hopes, dreams and expectations, and that I was justifiably angry. These strong emotions felt by all the members of our family had to be acknowledged and dealt with. Releasing them in a healthy and safe way is vital.

When I was in high school, I had a friend who introduced me to the art of journaling. She wrote pages and pages about what happened each and every day. She even gave me a journal with a small key so that I could lock my thoughts away. But as time went on, I did not want to lock my thoughts away, I wanted to bring them out in the open. In this situation, journaling became my safe release.

Over my ten-year healing journey, I brought into the open many feelings that I had kept bottled up inside; again, it was like emptying the forty-gallon drum teaspoon by teaspoon. Each teaspoon of hurt, pain and anger that was emptied was valid, and I gave myself permission to feel it as I released it to God. This went hand-in-hand with a process of forgiveness. I had to stop making excuses and sweeping what I felt under the carpet, and start expressing my true feelings instead.

Some people have shoved what they really think and feel inside for so long that it suddenly explodes like a volcano (or oozes out in snide remarks). This is an unhealthy expression of emotions and only ends up damaging you and those around you. If you want to move forward, you must validate your feelings, acknowledging and expressing your emotions in healthy way. Take a moment to express what you really think and feel using one of these ideas:

- Bring them to God in prayer if you are a person of faith
- Use a creative outlet such as painting, writing or music
- Talk to a trusted friend or support person
- Allow yourself to cry
- Verbalize your feelings aloud
- While you walk, throw rocks and specifically state how you feel
- Release emotional stress through physical exercise

These are just a few thoughts on what you can do to validate your feelings, but there are many resources that offer additional techniques. Remember, your pain is *your* pain, no matter how significant or insignificant you think it is. It is a worthwhile investment of time and energy to acknowledge it and deal with it so that you can move forward. Do not let unprocessed pain hold you back!

Allow yourself to grieve

Take time to grieve the loss of the life you expected. It is a real loss. Needless to say, it is very important to acknowledge and allow yourself the time and space to grieve. It is all a part of the healing journey and allows you to move forward so that you can have a hope-filled future.

Take responsibility

Only you can make the decision to move forward. We all need to take personal responsibility for how we respond to the circumstances in which we find ourselves. Perhaps your situation is toxic and requires drastic action. You may need to consider distancing yourself or, in extreme cases, leaving a particular relationship. However, for many people, evaluating their current circumstances (their 'here') enables them (usually with support) to make the changes necessary to move on to 'there'.

A key decision could be to take responsibility for seeking out support. For me it was enrolling in a course; for others, it might be weekly therapy. I also took responsibility to ensure that my family members had the support they required to deal with our stressful situation. This all does not happen by itself; appointments have to be made and kept, finances considered and prioritised. At times, it was easy to feel resentful about the money we spent on therapy or personal support. In our minds, we could have been using that money for a holiday. We had to sometimes seek out discounted supports or payment plans. Overall, though, I have found that when someone genuinely wants to receive help and take responsibility for moving forward, help is available irrespective of any limitations with regards to cost and time. Things have a way of working out!

Once we decide to take responsibility, we must consider the actions we need to take to enable that to happen. Here are some suggestions:

1. Face the fear

Fear keeps raising its ugly head. At least, it does for me; it will probably keep popping up as I release this book because, in my opinion, fear is the number one obstacle that prevents a person from moving forward from 'here' to 'there'! However, we have a saying: "Do it afraid!" In other words, don't shrink back because of fear. Do it anyway—despite the fear.

I have worked a lot on fear over my lifetime, and every time I think I have it under control, I become aware again how it is driving me. Once, I really wanted to take the bull by the horns and face fear head on. Though I am afraid of heights, I booked myself on a zipline course, thirty metres above the forest floor. I had to climb up very high trees and sit on the edge of a platform strapped into a harness, and then be pushed off by the instructor only to land on the next platform. Justin was strapped onto my lap, and we were both terrified. My whole body was shaking, and Justin wet his pants on me. But you know what, I 'did it afraid' and we both made a big step towards conquering our fear that day.

Justin went on to tackle diving boards at the local pool and abseiling in his outdoor education classes. But the greatest lesson this taught us was that we *can* do it afraid. These are my four top tips for facing your fears:

- Literally, face your fear; don't run and hide from it
- Let your fear roll over you rather than struggling and resisting it
- Be prepared to let time pass, and recognize that facing

fear will be a process
- Deal with setbacks related to your fear, and refuse to allow them to deter you

Is fear holding you back? What are you afraid of? Make a list of all your fears. Then find what stops you from facing them and determine to meet that challenge head on!

2. Take strategic risks

In the world of travel, you'll hear the saying, "If you never ever go, you will never ever know."

A life of pain, chaos and uncertainty can become an all-too-familiar scenario, and it can be tempting to stay where you are rather than risking moving forward. We can become comfortable with discomfort, as that is what feels familiar and safe. The reality is that with any risk, your efforts may not turn out the way you had hoped.

For example, I thought that once I progressed through my years of healing and recovery, we might have the opportunity to move to another community, with a new job and a fresh start. Truthfully, there is nothing wrong with the community I have been part of for twenty-six years or the area where we live; I really could not have asked for more. It has been exactly what we needed as we raised our family. However, for me at least, our journey of healing also created a strong desire for change.

I have been more than willing to leave the familiar and move into something new, and so has Ian. But the opportunity never presented itself, and we continue to be planted in our familiar community. We are at peace that this is where we are meant to be for now. The risk of relocating was not one our family has had to take.

Over the years, people have asked why it seems I cope so well. When I explain a little of what I have invested in my own healing and development, I am met with "I could never do that" and the excuses start coming. But when we take ownership of our lives and our response to pain before God, we can experience deep restoration. We are like an unrenovated house that needs to have the junk cleaned out of all the rooms. When our lives are cleared of the mess, freshly swept and given a coat of paint, we become like a newly-restored house. We become an inviting place for others to move towards.

I believe this cleaning out process is ultimately worth the work. Once we discover and deal honestly with the roots of our dysfunctional coping strategies (which may have festered over many years) we are truly able to discover who we really are. It's a risk worth taking!

3. Stay connected

Difficulties tend to isolate people from family and friends but it is important to remain connected to community. When life gets tough, it can seem like your world is closing in around you and no one understands what you are going through. When I was barely surviving, struggling to keep my head above water, I decided to remain connected in the best ways I could. That meant maintaining links with my church family, keeping some work, developing myself in my career and accepting help even if it did not feel like much was achieved by doing so. It all contributed to keeping me connected.

That old saying, 'out of sight, out of mind' is very true. The more I withdrew and did not appear to be 'doing' anything, the more it felt I was being left behind. I needed to strike a balance between setting boundaries and pruning back on activities that consumed valuable time and energy versus choosing to attend or join groups which were supportive of our situation. For example, when I connected with friends at the course I attended each month, it came with the added bonus of lifelong friendships. We journeyed together in person for four years, but years later, we still meet up online. At times it felt like it was too exhausting to remain connected, but by choosing to hang in there, even by a thread, we were given a valuable source of relationship that is essential for a person's well-being.

Take some time to write down all your connections. Are there people in your life with whom you could rekindle a relationship? Are there groups you could join that you have brushed off due to feeling overwhelmed by time constraints? If you have become disconnected, what steps could you take to enable you to form stronger relationships and develop a support system?

4. Step out and trust

Ultimately, it is up to you to step out, take the risk, face the pain and learn to trust that God will do immeasurably more than you can ask or imagine. It is a step of faith because the way forward can be fraught with all kinds of twists and turns. You'll encounter both mountains and valleys, but God is faithful. When I stepped out in faith, it was not all smooth sailing. Family relationships were not restored the way I desired, my marriage was still a work in progress, and I was still in the same routine with the same responsibilities each week, and so on.

I was expecting immediate external changes that would ease the pressure and strain of all that I had on my plate. But it was unrealistic of me to think that all the responsibilities that come with raising a family would disappear. It was me who had to change and examine how I responded to my situation; accepting that we are the ones who need to change takes both courage and faith. The reality was that a transformation was happening from the inside out, and it started with me. I can't make others become what they don't want to become. I can put in the work from my end, but, ultimately, I have to trust that as I remain faithful to what God has called me to do as a wife and mother and in my other roles, He will bring the chaos into order. Can you step out and trust that as you do your bit, God will do His? Let's choose to believe that He can and will do immeasurably more than we ask or imagine!

Chapter Eight

How to Become Unstuck

As a special needs mother, I often feel stuck. What other mothers do for their kids without even blinking, like enrolling them in a class or finding a coach to teach a skill, might, for me, involve weeks or even years of conversations so that my son can have the same opportunities as other young people. I feel stuck when the waiting lists for therapy are horrendously long or when he isn't included in a social engagement. Special needs people and their families are often passed over, which is difficult to navigate.

The reality is, if I do not advocate for Justin, who will? When you have a child with additional needs, you become that child's voice. Sometimes this is misunderstood by the broader community as the parent being pushy, self-centred, and consumed by their situation. Rather than offering support, people can assume the family's expectations are too high and feel resentful, even of the special needs child. Often, we are perceived as constantly pushing to break through the obstacles that stand in the way of our children's progress.

No parent should have to fight so hard for their child to receive the help they need, yet sadly this is all too common, and many families simply do not have the energy to continue and give up. One of the most common things I hear is that people are too exhausted to struggle any longer. Families capitulate, and they (as well as their child) do not receive what they need to progress.

I am thankful that slowly but surely in many countries, things are changing as people are becoming better educated and resourced to enable special needs families to thrive instead of just survive. Mindsets are slowly changing as children are being included in mainstream schools. I'm thankful that *yes* is now a more common word than *no*. However, there is still a long way to go, and it is not uncommon to feel stuck over and over again. Being stuck creates a feeling of hopelessness and, for hope to win, there must be regular support and opportunities available for every member of the special needs family. Just coming out of the house and being in community is a big step forward. Needy families are often hidden away, and others are unaware of the benefits of community on their wellbeing. A supportive church family has been essential for us to remain connected and engaged in wider society.

Families with additional needs often feel like they are spectators in life instead of participants. For example, I was struck as I was walking down the beach at Mum's the other day by how carefree and happy a group of wind surfers were as they whipped across the white tips of the waves on their boards. I looked at them longingly, desiring to be where they were as I walked the long stretch of beach. I was a spectator from my vantage point of the sand and received some pleasure from watching them surf, but I was by no means participating in their experience. This is what each day is like for many families of children with physical or mental health needs so consuming that they separate the family from mainstream society. People in these situations can see what others have, but it seems impossible to attain it. The uphill battle can seem too hard, and hopelessness sets in.

I encourage you, my dear reader, if you have made it this far, please do not give up, there is hope and a way forward. Even if you focus on just one of the points below for as long as you need, you are making progress. The old saying is true: *How do you eat an elephant? One piece at a time.* So, let us continue moving onwards slowly but surely. Remember it is okay to be a tortoise instead of a hare in this journey of becoming unstuck! Take heart! Progress is always being made, even when you think it is not. It is helpful, however, to identify the areas where you feel stuck:

1. Mindset

Your mindset can prevent you from progressing. Take time to identify and write down beliefs that might be keeping you stuck, such as: "Things will never change", "Our situation is hopeless, what is the point in trying?", "There is no future for us", or "The odds are stacked against us."

2. Circumstances

No matter your situation right now, circumstances change. Where you are now is likely not where you will be in the future. However, it is important to acknowledge your current location. Write down what life looks like for you today and why you feel stuck. Then determine what is preventing you from moving forward, with a view to changing those circumstances you're not happy with.

3. Attitudes of others

Sometimes it is the unspoken thoughts and responses others have towards us that get us down. It is not always what people say, but what they do not say that hinder us. Non-verbal judgements can come across as a patronising pat on the shoulder, a sickly-sweet tone of voice, or a facial expression. Perhaps people talk about including you, but you find out later you have not been included. The reality is that some people may not really care about your circumstances.

Look at who you choose to surround yourself with. Are they people who seek to understand and support you in your situation? Do they demonstrate care and concern, or do they simply pity and look down on you? If you have relationships like this, it may be time to re-evaluate them and build a new support base—believe it or not, understanding and caring people are out there!

4. Finances

Finances can be an area of significant struggle for special needs families. The expenses associated with special needs can be astronomical, even with government funding. If your finances are in trouble, it is important to act. Organisations exist that can help if this is an area where you feel stuck. Christians Against Poverty one such organisation; they partner with local churches to provide vital debt counselling and budgeting to families. Seek out support in your local community by finding an organisation that is able to offer hope and a financial pathway forward.

5. Trusted Support

Once of the most difficult issues special needs families face is accessing reliable respite support with a team that can be trusted.

There is no easy answer to this one, but stick with it and persevere until you find the team that you are seeking. I have had several teams of people involved with my son over the years, and it has taken quite some time and effort at each stage of his life to find the right people. This is an area that can place significant stress on special needs families. If the right support workers are not found, it impacts your ability to work, have your child attend their appointments, and achieve their goals. Therefore, your child's and your own personal well-being is at risk. Support workers often receive low wages, which causes inadequacies in the system—such as workers who are unqualified for the job or unmotivated to do it well.

This is where I can sincerely say that it is my faith in God that has enabled me to become unstuck in this situation. Each time Justin needs a new support worker, I ask God to bring the right person. Each time He has, and they have usually given us a number of years of service. But I have had to search thoroughly to find them and assure myself that they will be suitable for Justin.

6. Caregiver Roles

It can be challenging when you find yourself stuck in a caregiver's role, perhaps due to lack of an adequate support team. As a mother, you expect the role of caregiver to diminish over time, until you are freed up. But for the parents of a special needs child, this is often not the case. This means not only is there caregiver fatigue to battle, but also the feeling that you are indefinitely stuck in that role. This is why it is important to work out how to avoid losing yourself in this role as I did when I abandoned my love of music. You may be a caring and nurturing person, but it is important to have balance in your life and retain that sense of who you are.

THE WAY OUT

Getting stuck is easy. Getting unstuck is hard. But even if your circumstances do not change, I have learned that there are ways to make progress. Here are several strategies I use when I feel like I'm 'up against a wall,' and powerless to change my circumstances:

Determine the root of the problem. It is easy to fall into the trap of trying to deal with surface issues by putting band-aids on them. For example, we may try to sooth our pain with bubble baths, drinks or comfort eating. A better option is to take the time to identify why we feel stuck, and take specific action.

Do not procrastinate. Once you have identified the issues which cause you to feel stuck, face them one at a time. The longer you delay, the longer you will be in the same place!

Do your part. This can be very difficult because fear patterns can be so entrenched, and we would rather avoid situations than have to face our fear. But it is walking through the fear that eventually eliminates it. Fear loses its power when we are no longer afraid of it. Just as our legs cannot function without the impulses from the brain that move the nerves and muscles, so we need to be empowered in our faith by our Heavenly Father. This is why I believe having faith in God is so important in this journey.

Know when to stop. Life sometimes feels like a giant brick wall in front of you that, no matter how hard you push, will not budge. I am a pusher. I grew up with the saying, "where there is a will, there is a way". Sometimes, I have to know when to stop pushing and trust that I have done everything I can to progress the situation and now need to sit back and see how it unfolds.

Know that it's okay to take 'no' for an answer. I hate to take 'no' for an answer; I like to find the answer to every problem. But it is exhausting to live as though it is always up to me to solve every problem. Becoming the 'burden bearer' is what made me feel weighed down by the challenges we faced with Justin's situation. Realise that it is acceptable to choose your battles, and know when to say 'enough is enough', and then let go.

Never give up on what matters. God wants us to soar like eagles, not be stuck in a claustrophobic chicken coop like a battery hen. Jesus raised the dead, and His love and power is undiminished today. Still, those who had been raised had to get back up on their feet and walk! Though our circumstances may not change, we can always make small adjustments towards what seems to be most important. Each of those adjustments, no matter how insignificant or small they seem, ultimately adds up to progress. When you look back and see all the steps you have taken, you will discover that your family is no longer in the same place you once were.

Chapter Nine

Grit & Determination

Grit is a character trait based on an individual's perseverance combined with the passion for a particular long-term goal. Caring for a special needs family member is a mission for a tortoise, not a hare. It is grit and determination that are required to go the distance!

So, what role do grit and determination play in moving into a life of hope and purpose? I wish a magic wand could be waved over our circumstances, or that God would step down and resolve all the challenges immediately. However, in my experience, that's just not how it works. I do believe in miracles and have no doubt that they happen. However, for whatever reason, I do not often see God's immediate, dramatic intervention. I believe this is because He is more interested in our journey and who we are becoming than in immediate end results.

This is not because God enjoys our suffering; in fact, the Bible makes it clear that He has great compassion for human suffering. But God uses our suffering to draw us closer to Him, and also help us become more compassionate, sensitive, realistic, and in tune with ourselves and the needs of those around us. Nothing we go through is wasted; every experience, good or bad, can be used to help others as they traverse similar territory. Our lives are never about just us.

The reality is that it does take a measure of true grit and determination to decide to affect positive change in desperate situations—particularly when the world may deem our problems as hopeless or resign us to living on the sidelines. I do not think it is too much to ask that our story ends well.

In Australia, much work has been done in the area of disability by the government and advocacy groups to change the expectation of the quality of life for disabled people. However, from my experience, many churches are still a long way from being able to offer the support that special needs families require to easily connect into a local church community. It remains challenging for Christians with special needs children to remain in the church. The family must make an intentional decision to stay connected despite the challenges that will arise.

In many ways, we must be pioneers in our own situations. In our home state, Justin was one of the first participants to receive the National Insurance Disability Scheme funding. We took Justin for all of his therapy assessments, and our occupational therapist wrote compelling reports outlining Justin's needs in the home. It took time before our need for home modifications became evident, but we soon discovered these changes could make a big difference, not only to Justin, but to our entire family. These modifications enabled Justin to take responsibility more easily and safely for his daily living which decreased the pressure on the rest of us. When we moved to our current home, Justin's needs were not fully apparent, so we had not taken this into account. After occupational therapist assessments, however, it became clear to Ian and me that our house was not suitable. There were so many impediments to Justin's independence and safety, from a gas cooktop, to thin glass shower screens, to mirrored cupboard doors, to the number of keys we needed to unlock the front door . . . the list went on. These barriers created learned helplessness in Justin; he felt there was no use trying when even the simple things in life were too hard.

When Justin was set up for success, we were all able to move on. But whenever we encountered roadblocks in Justin's situation, all of our lives come to a grinding halt, and pressures and tensions started to surface in our family relationships. Feeling like you can move only as fast as the weakest member of the family is incredibly frustrating! They say patience is a virtue, and for us, it is certainly something that we have had to develop.

During this season in our life, we had a low cash flow. The cost of household renovations was beyond us, so when we discovered that there was funding for home modifications, we were hopeful and experienced a real feeling of relief and hope for the future. However, with any new program comes all the teething problems. In the excitement of a new scheme being rolled out, the planners were too generous and kind, and gave false hope to participants. We were promised more than the plan could realistically provide, and the following year, cutbacks kicked in. It was an added stress to have that hope of support later reduced, particularly in the area of home modifications.

Before Justin was diagnosed, I had never been a goal setter. Now, I find it essential to make lists. Ian and I sat down and wrote a list of ideal home modifications, and then imagined what it would be like to have everything on it. We could feel the stress lifting as we imagined not having to worry about Justin falling through the shower screen, or not having to purchase a new bed every few months or have our son sleep on a mattress on the floor. But as our imagining went on, all we could see were dollar signs and a staggering amount of work to be done. We needed a long-term plan if we were to make our home user-friendly for Justin, especially as he transitioned into adulthood. The way forward in this situation has required grit and determination, and I have had to become a grittier person than I ever thought I could be. But though it has been extremely challenging, thanks to the significant input and support of so many people, we have made significant progress towards reaching these goals.

Home Goals

If you have longer-term goals that would make an enormous difference in your family life, I encourage you to not give up on them. External goals are as important as personal wellbeing goals because they impact the whole family's wellbeing.

Here are some tips to start the ball rolling to make your goals a reality:

1. Write a dream list for your home. Do you need handrails, more robust furniture, rearrangement of living spaces, bathroom or kitchen modifications, or sensory garden spaces, for example?

2. Keep up with therapist reports and have regular home assessments so that they can support your claims.

3. Share your child's needs with supportive family and friends and accept their help. For example, my brother designed and constructed an indestructible bed using his engineering background, which has been amazing!

4. Enlist a project planner or support coordinator to help bring it all together. We had a 'pathway meeting' with key people in Justin's life where we dreamt together about what needed to happen logistically to take him from 'here' to 'there'. This person worked with our family for years, overseeing our renovations and modifications, which took the pressure off Ian and me.
5. Use funding where possible, and find ways to achieve what funding will not cover.
6. Tackle one modification at a time. Even if only one or two spaces are fixed up each year, it makes a difference. Eventually, your house will meet the needs of your child and family.

By strategizing, we work out how to navigate tricky situations. This is an essential part of cultivating hope. Make the time to seek the advice of therapists. Talk through what is needed from their perspective. It is well worth the investment of time. Once your child's unique goals are clear, you may be ready to hold a family meeting.

Family Meetings

A family meeting aims to solve problems that make it difficult for the family to support a special needs person and to agree on a way forward. It is an opportunity to mind-map a path for the child and their family, as they all live in one house. A 'pathway session' highlights the needs of other family members, and enables those to be met as well.

In Australia, the focus on funding for special needs families is all about the participant's goals. Very little is geared toward the caregivers and family members who are impacted by the high demands of the person with the disability. This can create stressful situations. For example, when we were discussing bathroom modifications with our home assessors, we were told that Ian and I should move out of our bedroom as it had an ensuite. They felt we should use the shared bathroom with our other two children so that Justin could have the ensuite space in our house. I understood why that recommendation was made, but we felt that there it lacked consideration for the other four people in our family, let alone our privacy as a couple. It takes determination to not just roll over and have everybody else's life negatively affected in order to access funding.

In this case, it took many firm conversations for Ian and me to navigate a suitable solution. A compromise was eventually made, and the main bathroom was fully renovated to disability standards. Grit and determination were required to ensure some sort of balance within the family unit so that everyone's needs were being met—even if one person required a higher level of accommodation.

Holding a pathway session means that all family members can have a voice, including siblings who can work with the support team to come up with solutions to some of the imbalances, and express how they feel. While the disabled person bears no fault, the impact of their needs on the family is a reality. Clearly stating the issues and then seeking solutions to solve them generates hopefulness rather than hopelessness. Daily living can improve for all family members, not just the person with special needs.

If it is challenging to engage a support organisation to run a pathway session, consider initiating and running one yourself. The best way to do this is to gather key people and family together. Before the meeting, it is best to prepare by:

1. Nominating a pathway coordinator to steer the conversation. This may be a therapist or someone from a carer support group who understands the needs of special needs families. Some providers offer a similar service for a fee.
2. Having somewhere to brainstorm together — long sheets of paper pinned to the wall (and suitable pens to write with), or an electronic notepad projected onto a screen so everyone can see.
3. Choosing the venue; the family's home may be easiest.
4. Setting a time limit of no more than two hours.
5. Providing afternoon tea (consider asking attendees to bring a plate).
6. Giving plenty of notice about the date and purpose of the meeting so that key people can attend. Include family members in the session as well as the special needs child if that is possible and suitable.

Family meetings are best held at critical transition times in a young person's life and can occur in the context of home or school. While they are helpful in terms of getting everyone on the same page and coming up with a coordinated approach, accountability and follow up are essential.

Looking Ahead

For a long time, our family could not see beyond each day. With the mindfulness movement currently being all the rage, where people are encouraged to live in the moment, it may be tempting to adopt that as a long-term solution. I understand the importance of taking a deep breath, of being aware of the here and now, and connecting in the moment. Sometimes this is all you and your family may feel able to do. However, setting achievable, longer-term goals beyond simply making it through each day cultivates hope that your situation will not always be exactly as it is now. Though your loved one may still be in a wheelchair or have autism or whatever their condition is, your family can still have a hope-filled life.

A mother once said to me after she found full-time care and support for her daughter with very high needs, "She has the best life; she can enjoy so many activities that I don't have time for!" It may take all your time and energy during this particular season to enable your child's goals so that they can step into their future. Still, when it comes together, it is a win for everyone.

Getting from where you are now to where you all want to be can happen. Over time, things do have a way of coming together if you don't give up. There will be injustices. Others may not understand why your drive and focus is all about your child and not others. But remember those wise words of Dr Seuss, "Unless someone like you cares a whole awful lot, nothing is going to get better. It's not." Who will be that person who cares 'a whole awful lot' if it's not you?

Chapter Ten

GRAPPLING WITH INJUSTICE

Life is not fair! Some people seem to start their lives with a silver spoon in their mouths. However, many people start out from a place of being underprivileged. Everything seems to be stacked against them from birth, from genetics to health to educational opportunities to a lack of wealth.

I am acutely aware that I am writing this book from the perspective of an Australian middle-class mother. I have all the governmental supports and systems which are available in my country, yet we still struggle. I am grieved by the injustice towards disabled people here, let alone in countries where there is little if any value placed on the lives of the disabled. I know people in other countries who have to fund every ounce of support and therapy for their disabled family member. Sometimes other family members take the initiative to start not-for-profit organisations, employing therapists and hosting respite programs which benefit their own child and many others. But often the situation is desperate. A friend of mine in India has a nonverbal young-adult family member with severe autism. During the Covid-19 pandemic, they have been locked away in an apartment from dawn till dusk, as the country has been in lockdown. Their young man rarely sleeps, and the family has the pressure of coping with his verbal tics and stimming (self-stimulation, usually in the form of repetitive movements such as rocking) with no breaks, as there are no support services. Not being able to go outside is tough, let alone when you are a full-time caregiver for a disabled person.

How is a situation like this fair? The reality is that each of us has their own pain. Whether you are raising special needs children in a middle-class home in Australia or on the brink of poverty in India, suffering exists in both cases. How we respond to that suffering can make an enormous difference in how we handle life and how included special needs families feel in their communities. In some places, especially developing countries, the lack of support and the stigma of having a disability makes it easy to fall into a pit of hopelessness. This is why we must highlight these issues and advocate for change for special needs families and their children.

A special needs family's response to injustice is critical in determining how they will move forward. No matter what the starting point is, applying even some of the ideas in this book may help families to progress. Dealing with the strong feelings that come from living with injustice is essential for healing. It is not uncommon to experience persistent feelings of anger toward the unjust circumstances that often occur.

Caregivers and family members are often not angry with the special needs individual; more likely, they're angry about the unjust responses of others. They might be angry about the lack of access to support that would make a difference to everyone's quality of life, or angry at God for having allowed disability to be part of their family. Letting go of this anger is tough because the feeling seems justified. The physical limitations and restrictions placed upon people with disabilities and their families can cause much frustration as people are prevented from living the life they desire to lead.

The reality is that no one else can deal with those feelings for us! We need to recognise that many things may never change, however, we can gain control over the feelings we have in response to the injustices of disability and keep it from hurting our health and robbing us of happiness.

Promote Inclusion

Those who are visibly different from others are often excluded socially. People may feel awkward and not know how to include or talk with a person with a disability. For example, our son flaps, stims and has a tic disorder. The vocal tic means that he may hum and make unusual sounds, and he finds it very difficult to be still. He needs to move often and will jump up randomly, without consideration for his surroundings. In a quiet library, this can be socially awkward!

From the outside, Justin may be considered disruptive; people may presume he can help his behaviour and be more aware of what is happening around him. The reality is that he can, but only with enormous concentration. This takes all his energy and focus; it exhausts him, so it is unsustainable. As a result, people often think that he is not able to hold an intelligent conversation and dismiss him. The impact is that Justin is not always included in conversations or social groups, or chosen for group activities. This can create a wound of rejection in the special needs person leading to further anger.

Sadly, these scenarios then flow onto other family members when they are subconsciously pitied and looked down on by others. Well-meaning people using an almost patronising voice have stroked or patted my shoulder and commented they do not know 'how I do it'. I have found this very hard to process because I need friends, and I want to be seen as a woman in my own right, not only as the mother of a special needs person. I have also felt passed over in my career and social opportunities when it is assumed that 'I have too much on my plate,' which I do. Still, the stimulation of being included actually gives me a new lease on life.

I have often felt like I have the same issues as my child, that because I gave birth to him, I am seen through the same lens. Though this may seem dramatic, this is how it has felt for me as I personally struggle with learning how to live with rejection. It is not what people say, but what they don't say, and the invitations they never offer.

Building an inclusive community is essential for the healing and wellbeing of special needs people and their families. We have been incredibly blessed to have become part of an inclusive church community who have unconditionally accepted and loved our son. This has been instrumental to his emotional well-being and has enabled hope for his own future. The young adults have included him on their leadership team and have opened up their lives to him and vice versa. Even if a church has no idea about how to handle families with disabilities except to love them, this really is the key. No one at our church is fazed if Justin jumps up in the middle of a service or calls out; they simply let it happen and move on. And as parents, we do not need to feel embarrassed because that church community loves and accepts him for who he is, and understands how he behaves.

Take Responsibility

Everyone needs to take responsibility for including others. This can be done in various ways:

Provide a supportive environment. For example, when my friend's children were diagnosed with autism, our church put locks on the front door so she could enjoy a cup of tea after the service without having them running out on the road.

Create a can-do culture. Rather than seeing all the work or what appears to be impossible, look for what is possible. We did not think we could make the adjustments to our home, given our budget, but when we started having conversations with people and sharing our needs, we received helpful input and ideas about how we could make things work.

Be a visionary. The sky is the limit. If you allow yourself to dream and imagine what would make a difference in these people's lives, it can become reality! Create an environment and awareness of all people with a disability. This will enhance the quality of not only their interactions and friendships, but also yours as you foster connections among a rich, diverse community of people who may never have connected otherwise.

Reach out. Offering to support families with special needs can be rewarding and enable you to have a greater understanding of the similarities and differences among people.

Invest in equipment, modifications, or adaptations. Be willing to modify or adapt spaces so that special needs friends can visit or participate in activities. Search for low-cost ways to do this. For example, you might change the door lock to a touchpad or purchase a small ramp to make it easy for wheelchairs to enter the building.

Define What's Not Worth It

As a special needs family member, try not to keep looking back. It changes nothing! You need to decide it is not worth holding onto injustice, or it will take over your life. One of the hardest things I have had to come to terms with is that most people are so focused on their own lives and issues that they do not look outside of themselves to even realise what another person is going through. This is why it is so essential to become people who care because, when people care, things get better!

We can lift others out of the pit with us when we take the time to share our story and struggle. By staying focused on your situation, your child's condition and the rejection you regularly experience, you are hurting only yourself. No one else is stewing over your plight; they are all getting on with their lives!

But be kind to and patient with yourself. Recognising that you are doing your best and that it is okay to make time for self-care, will leave less room for anger. I used to feel guilty if I spent money on myself. Then I learned that the self-care of having a massage or a beauty treatment can take the edge off the stress. It nurtured me and made my emotions seem less intense. Even a good long soak in the bath can reduce negative feelings. Relaxation is essential when it comes to diffusing the intensity of those feelings.

Ask "What Would Jesus Do?"

My faith in God helped me as I went to Him for comfort and reassurance. Even when others may not see or understand my pain, it is comforting to know that He does and that He also understands injustice. From a faith perspective, it can be helpful to realise that Jesus suffered much injustice. He was rejected by many people in

His day. But He was also accepted by those who were unacceptable to society. The religious leaders of the day hoped for a Messiah to enact justice. They wanted Jesus to come and kick the Romans out of leadership and end their oppression. However, did they really want to have Jesus insist on the establishment of a fair and just system? Were they really concerned that the basic needs of all humans were met? The heart of Jesus was to enact justice by reaching out to the broken, disenfranchised and lost, and to speak out on their behalf. He was a friend to the friendless and a voice to the voiceless.

When you suffer injustice, it's difficult to show love and resist lashing out in anger. I have often struggled with this. As I hit brick wall after brick wall and felt like I was not being heard, I wanted to demand my rights. It is challenging to deal with constant misunderstanding and injustice, especially when you are seeking to have basic human needs met. Advocacy takes an emotional toll.

I have had to keep myself in check by taking deep breaths and making sure that I do not allow my emotions to get out of control, especially while I am explaining my situation to care providers, school staff, or support workers. Ian urges me to guard my demeanour; he tells me that when I get stressed about injustice, I am not a very likeable person. I feel injustice profoundly, and it's difficult to avoid strong reactions when I have to fight so hard for progress.

However, it is never acceptable to take our frustration out on others, especially when they are trying to help. Frustration occurs on both sides when agencies are poorly funded and support workers are underpaid. When I see signs in government agencies saying that aggressive behaviour will not be tolerated, I am never surprised. Injustice brings out the worst in people, even when their frustration is justified.

What did Jesus really do?

- He displayed love to everyone by embracing the excluded.
- He challenged cultural practices and unjust behaviours without sinning.
- He rejected exclusive actions and protested inequality.
- He risked His reputation to walk alongside the outcasts of society.

What can I do?

- I can take responsibility for my own response to injustice and choose to respond well to others.
- I can love others to the best of my ability.
- I can treat others how I want to be treated.
- I can be kind to myself and take the injustices to God.
- I can let go of injustice and try to not hold others to account when they do not understand.

While it is true that life is unfair, we must deal with the injustice we encounter in order to help others. Justice matters. It matters to God, and it should matter to us. It is perfectly normal to feel angry over injustice, but we must use that anger productively to raise awareness of the problem. Highlight the need in your community, raise funds to support people with disabilities, and demonstrate compassion whenever possible.

Kindness also matters. So many good causes need our help and support. For example, some organisations build homes for the disabled so that they can have independent living accommodation. Others install ramps in public places so that physically disabled people can enjoy a meal or sensory spaces in playgrounds.

Use your negative energy towards injustice for good; seek out those in need, and help others as you would like to be helped. I did this by starting a playgroup which included disabled kids in my community. I knew what exclusion felt like, and I did not want other mothers to feel isolated like we did. Some people with an interest in disability care have started podcasts that offer hope and encouragement.

Balance is the key. You have to pick your battles, as you will not win every one you face. Maybe you will have to compromise on a home modification or accept less funding or not have your child in the school of your choice. Ultimately, carefully choose where you decide to stand your ground. Remain as objective as possible, try to understand why you are being blocked, and then systematically and calmly remove the blockages. Often the blocks are there because others are afraid of what will happen if they say 'yes'. Sometimes there is simply a communication breakdown with key decision-makers unable to say 'yes' in case it sets a precedent they cannot maintain.

Not every battle is worth the emotional toll or investment of our time. However, many are because, when you do win, you are winning on behalf of the other special needs families who will not have to fight because you did. They may receive the home modification, the placement at the school, inclusion in a particular community group or course, and so on. You will have paved the way and provided hope for others. It may have been costly to you on many levels, but it is always worth it when hope wins!

Chapter Eleven

Managing Time, Finances & Holidays

I cannot escape the feeling that some of my readers may think it is unrealistic to accomplish all that I have been discussing. I will be honest, it is challenging, and managing time can be one of the biggest impediments to cultivating hope in your family life. But don't let that stop you. Remember, how do you eat an elephant? One bite at a time!

Get Organised

Some days when I feel pushed in all directions, I remember one of my husband's sayings: "Just let me chase one rabbit down a hole at a time". Ian prefers a single focus; he likes to take one task at a time and see it through to completion. We all have different personality types, and some lend themselves to being more organised and managing time better than others. If you don't know your personality type, I suggest that you choose a test (Myers Briggs, for example) and discover what your type is. I took a test before I had children, and I was a 'Diplomat' on the Myers Briggs chart. I was weak at administration, not great at time management and did not see myself ever working in an office. I was much more relational, enthusiastic and creative. However, as the demands of raising a special needs child increased, I was forced to become more and more organised.

Spreadsheets and I are still not the best of friends, but I am beginning to warm to them. I had to learn to manage time better in order to survive. Families with special needs children either sink or swim when the demands of appointments and managing support teams and finances all come piling in. Still, research is clear that the best chance for special needs children to progress happens with consistent early intervention in the child's first years. So, how do you find the time amongst all the other competing needs of daily life?

Manage Your Time

The role of a special needs parent requires a set of skills that other parents may never need to fully develop. I used to resent this, but as I moved through the grieving process, I started to embrace the newfound skills I was developing. I decided to use them professionally, as well as in my family. I began to put my hand up at work for leadership roles, because that was what I was learning at home. As a result, I was promoted twice. Instead of resenting being buried in administration, I used it as an opportunity to learn, grow and develop even better time management skills. During the years I was more housebound, I wrote curriculum, focusing my energy on learning how to write well. I used this strategy to combat self-pity.

As a special needs mother, with so many things on my plate, I have to fight to be in a place where multitasking is not necessary. I don't have the luxury of saying, "Let me just chase one rabbit down a hole at a time". So, I evaluate how I am going to tackle my days so that my family and I can live well. There are many great resources to help kick start your planning!

In order to avoid feeling overwhelmed, I must be systematic in my approach to each day. Children, especially those with special needs, thrive on routine. I encourage you to develop a routine that provides opportunities for you to have a break in the day. Put your feet up with a cuppa. If you find this hard to do, ask for help. Enlist others to help you carry the load.

Finances

After one occupational therapy home assessment, it became apparent that, with Justin approaching adulthood, having an independent living space would enable him to develop the daily living skills necessary to achieve his personal goals. We felt we needed a unit in the basement of our home built to disability standards so that Justin could safely learn these skills and practice living independently with support. The outcome, however, was that funding would only be provided to renovate our usual living space. The assessors felt that living downstairs would be too isolating for Justin, but we really struggled with this decision as a family. We did not think it was best for Justin or for the rest of us.

We already had a caregiver who arrived at six thirty each morning to help with Justin's morning routine. But it was awkward having a caregiver in our house so early as we were trying to get ready for work and school. To give them space (and us, privacy), my husband, daughter, and I would have breakfast out most mornings. This created additional stress and tension in our already fragile family relationships, so we finally let go of the support.

What we really needed was an independent living space where caregivers could work with Justin privately. We ultimately decided it was worth it to personally fund this solution. For many, this kind of decision brings great financial strain. The costs to properly set up people with disabilities can be astronomical. For some families, this means the purchase of additional property or paying for supported living. Other family members may begin to resent the amount of money being spent on the person with additional needs, as they have to go without holidays or outings or sometimes even basic needs due to a lack of money. Families get weary from living under such financial strain, and it can break up even the strongest household.

If your finances have been negatively affected due to caring for a special needs family member, I encourage you to seek help before they go further downhill. Managing even the messiest of finances is possible, but you may need to find support. There are organisations who can sometimes provide money to assist or offer suggestions, like refinancing your home to a lower interest rate.

I once reached out to carers when we were at a really low ebb as a family and had not had a holiday in a long time. They had some spare funds and offered to pay for a beach house for us for a week. It was just what we needed to bring us back from the brink of breaking point. Finding help may require searching for funding or support to assist in times of crisis or great need. Don't give up!

Holidays

While holidays are good for all families from time to time, they are essential for families with additional needs. Taking some time away from the pressures of normal home life is vital for our well-being. Studies have shown that taking regular breaks reduces stress, minimises the risk of illness and improves overall health. A change from the usual routine can recharge our batteries. But the challenge of taking a holiday can be more stressful than simply staying at home! Planning the right holiday destination with appropriate accommodations well in advance is necessary if the holiday is to meet the needs of your whole family.

Whenever we spontaneously headed off for a holiday without pre-planning, we didn't have what we required for the needs of our family. This resulted in stress instead of the relaxation we needed. Therefore, I became intentional about scheduling holidays. Some were better than others, and it was trial and error. But we remained committed to getting away.

Finding the right accommodation was challenging. Many places don't accommodate special needs. For example, there may be no ramps, the location may be on busy roads, or the locking system isn't adequate for keeping children contained and safe. The furniture may have sharp edges, or therapy pets might not be welcome. I eventually made a list of what would and would not work for our family on holiday to make the search easier. We decided we needed:

- spacious accommodations so that the children can have their own room
- to be within walking distance of the beach or shops so we weren't in and out of the car frequently
- internet access
- to have linen provided
- a pool (swimming was my way of relaxing)

Determine ahead of time what does not work for your family and avoid those situations. I learned to avoid holidays where our family would have been confined to a small space. I didn't plan trips that would require us to be in crowded places or places that were not well equipped for Justin's needs. Decide the parameters you need to put in place to ensure that your family gets a break. Below are a few suggestions:

- Find a reliable travel agent to help you find suitable accommodation. Choose accommodations with on-site or in-room spa treatments and room service for the times when it is difficult to go out. Some places handle special needs better than others, so be sure to select those that best suit your family's needs.
- Do your research. Often theme parks or wildlife parks offer passes for families with special needs. Some allow special needs families to join a shorter queue for attractions. Others allow access to rides or theatres from a side entrance that is quieter and more spacious since noise and crowds are often triggering for a special needs child.
- Work out a savings plan and budget for holidays.
- Consider using respite care while you're on holiday. Look for programs that will provide for the special needs family member or find a caregiver who can come to the accommodation at times so your family can participate in activities that would not be optimal for your special needs child.

Two years ago, I visited my brother in the United Kingdom, whom I had not been to see in the twenty-plus years he had lived there. We had put off the visit due to the potential challenges of travelling overseas with a special needs child. We planned meticulously and navigated quite a few challenges. We arranged meet-and-greet services at each airport so we'd have quiet spaces to rest and to make going through customs as smooth as possible. This significantly reduced Justin's stress and anxiety due to the unfamiliar. I am so grateful for the people who volunteer to help families like ours at airports.

The medication Justin was taking at the time we travelled was an issue. Even though his medications are approved in Australia, not all of them were approved pharmaceuticals in the Middle East, where we were transiting. Therefore, I needed to arrange for scripts to be available in England to ensure Justin would have what he needed.

Before heading overseas, we also researched which venues were supportive of people with special needs and we tended to visit those to decrease the chances of our day being upended by a meltdown. Logistically it was a lot of work, but it was worth it, and in hindsight I am glad that we pushed through. The time management, financial and administrative skills that I had strengthened while raising Justin were key to us being able to pull off a family trip to see my brother. Slowly developing these skills to plan, save and take a holiday, paid off in the long run.

Recently, we have been putting those same skills to use as we prepared to transition Justin into life beyond school. The investment in time and effort is worth it! Use your time wisely and make the most of every opportunity to help move your family forward from your 'here' to your 'there'!

PART 3

Cultivating a Hope-Filled Life

Chapter Twelve

LEARNING TO TRUST

A critical part of cultivating hope is learning to trust, first in God and then in the people He places around you to support your child and family. I used to think I did not need any help, but I quickly realised that I needed to avail myself of the support others offered. The challenge was that I did not always trust the support workers assigned to us. I felt uncomfortable having strangers in our house and entrusting Justin into their care, even though they had been screened; to me, they often still seemed under-qualified and not always invested in the job. We had some poor experiences, and I struggled with not wanting to accept help.

As a result, I choose to self-manage Justin's funding so that Ian and I can have a say in who is caring for him and coming into our home. It takes time and energy to coordinate your child's support team, but it is well worth the investment. It is also valuble to source a reliable support coordinator under a self-managed plan, and a therapy assistant to ease the load of managing supports and outworking therapy routines at home. Having a person in these key roles may reduce the number of team members you need to communicate with and give back some time in your week for you. Without a trustworthy team, you will have to do everything yourself, which then leads to caregiver fatigue and possibly burnout. At some point, you have to rely on others. When you find the right people and begin to see your child's needs being met, it cultivates hope. It also helps you feel less alone in raising your child.

Here are a few keys to finding a trustworthy support team:

Do your research. Do not simply accept the first therapist that shows up on an internet search. Read reviews and contact others who have used the service the therapist offers. Some therapists might focus more on your child's particular need. For example, an occupational therapist may specialise in sensory, learning, or daily living, which may be more applicable to your child's needs than general occupational therapy.

Be prepared to change therapists if you don't feel your child's needs are being adequately met.

Request an interview or trial session. Do this before committing to the worker or form of support. Have an honest and open conversation about what the support person will offer and hear their thoughts on your child's needs.

Be prepared to sit on a waiting list and use interim support until the person you want becomes available.

Be consistent in turning up to appointments or keeping respite hours. If you regularly cancel, building a relationship is difficult. Appointments should be kept rain, hail, or shine, in order to build loyalty. Your support team will then prioritise you as a long-term client, which benefits your child, who will respond better as a history develops between the child and the support team.

Stick with a support worker or therapist who is a good fit for your family. This may mean that you have to rearrange some of your schedule to fit with theirs. It is worth the inconvenience, however, as it is much harder to find reliable support than rearrange a schedule.

Allow respite workers who have proven their reliability to take your child to appointments.

Request university students who are studying in the therapy fields in which your child is receiving therapy.

Regularly communicate with the support team via text, email or phone. If the respite worker takes your child to therapy, it is essential to keep that worker informed. This will help you to maintain a relationship with the team and reinforce therapy as required in the home.

Be patient; it takes time to build a relationship. If you are honest and open with people, it helps to create a rapport, and in turn, trust.

Pay accounts on time. Don't hire people you know you don't have the funds in the bank to pay; and make sure workers are paid on time to avoid issues over money.

Both you and the therapist must be honest when issues arise. If you feel the therapy is a waste of time because you are not seeing results, discuss that. If the therapist would like to see more follow up at home, that assessment should not be met with any resistance from the family. Honesty is essential so that issues can be resolved before they escalate.

It is the long-term commitment to therapy or treatment that will make all of the difference to your child's progress. A special needs child will find it harder to respond to therapy if the team is constantly changing. This can be challenging because we very much live in a world of high staff turnover. In my work in schools, I have seen how positive it is for students to get used to having an entire team of learning support assistants. This means they do not become overly dependent on just one or two people and then become anxious when those few are not available.

Drawing from my experience, I believe that it is vital to have a consistent team of people who know your family's story. This, I believe, is best worked out in the context of community. We made a deliberate choice to stay in the community where our children were born. Seeing the familiar faces of the same people in school, church, sports clubs, therapy, medical teams and even our local shops—people who all know Justin—is important. Over the years, trust builds, and I am quietly confident that others would look out for him should the need arise, because he is known in our area. This sense of community cultivates hope in people. As they say, it takes a village to raise a child and, in my opinion, that is especially true of a special needs child.

The issue of trust also goes much deeper than simply having a trustworthy support team. I will not deny that it can be extremely difficult to find people to build a team. Even when people are paid in disability support, the wages are low, and often it is not their first choice of work. So, it is difficult not to worry about who will care for my child or how to find the right specialist when they are all so busy and do not seem to need another patient. This is where a much deeper trust has to come in if we are not to give in to stress and anxiety.

Each time I lose a support worker or therapist who has been instrumental in Justin's life, I find it difficult to not be anxious. I know how hard they will be to replace and how time-consuming it may be to find the next one. I used to get terribly stressed about it.

Now I have learnt to give it over to God and trust in Him to bring the people we need into Justin's life. The Bible repeatedly talks about not being anxious, so it must be possible! It also says that God will provide for (or meet) all of our needs. If God promises to meet our needs, we need to trust that He will, no matter what our circumstances are!

I do not say this lightly because our needs are extensive. If they are not met, our lives are significantly impacted by increased pressure. Ian and I are restricted in what we can do to manage our day jobs. For example, we may not be able to attend meetings after work if we need to be the ones picking up Justin from school, or if there is no reliable transport driver who can take Justin to appointments.

Whatever your need for your child, present it to God. When we learn to move from a position of anxiety and fear to trust in Him who already knows what we need, it opens the door for God to meet the need. In my case, I choose to bring support workers, my lack of home modifications, and Justin's placement for future study, to God in prayer.

If I take matters into my own hands, try to make it all happen and become impatient, this may appear aggressive and demanding. If I want to get my own way, all it does is break down relationships, and people then do not want to support us. A delicate balance is needed when emotions and stress threaten to override reason and calm when you are seeking help. This applies even when you are in desperate need of support for your family.

I can remember crying on the phone to providers early in our journey. I would be pleading for help, as I could not balance caregiving and work, and I really did not want to give up my teaching job to be a full-time caregiver. The waiting lists were long, and it seemed impossible that I would receive the help I needed when so many were also needy. I did not want to feel like I was always the one pushing to get what we wanted, but I was also not at peace doing nothing. I think this is a struggle for many special needs families, as we are acutely aware that others may be in more desperate need than we are. Yet we all do need to advocate for our own child and family needs.

This is where having Christian faith has been invaluable for me. It helps me cope both mentally and emotionally. I have the choice to trust in God to take care of all the details. This means that I can literally hand over my problems for Him to solve, especially when I feel that anxiety and worry are about to overwhelm me.

A delicate balance must be sought between pursuing what is needed and trusting God to put all the pieces of the jigsaw puzzle together. God has the blueprint of what our lives and our children's lives look like, and He wants us to trust Him with how it unfolds. I have been learning to ask "What next, God?" because more often than not, I really do not know. Hope wins when deep trust in God grows. If you are a Christian and you want hope to be built in your life, I encourage you to work on developing trust in God. There are a number of ways you can do this:

1. Tell God how anxious or worried you are. Be real. He knows that we love our kids and want what is best for them. He also knows when we find it hard to see a way forward.

2. Write down what your impossible or difficult situation is.

3. Tell God what outcome you would like, and then release that outcome to Him.

4. Take responsibility and do your bit—make the phone call or appointment, have the conversation. Then, wait.

5. Get on with your life as you wait for the response. Focus on what you have in the here and now.

6. Bring it back to God if nothing has shifted. Like the persistent widow in a story Jesus once told, don't take 'no' for an answer! Start the steps again until there is a breakthrough

Most importantly, do not give up! When there are additional needs in a family, it is not uncommon to feel like prayers are hitting a brick wall, and it may be tempting to stop trying. But don't give up! No situation is impossible for God. Sometimes we need to accept that our solution or ideas for moving forward may not be what God knows is best. Remember He is the one with the blueprint for our lives. Isaiah 55:8-9 tells us that God's ways are not always our ways, and His thoughts are not our thoughts.

Once, after a time of personal healing and recovery, I thought that moving to a new location would be best for our family. In hindsight, I can see that it was better that I remain in my community and job, and keep things as stable as possible. I have realised that because we stayed in our community, Justin has been able to establish supportive and caring relationships with people who have known him over many years, and is familiar with his environment. My perspective eventually changed from feeling like I was being restricted, to understanding that we were actually freer to engage in community and daily life because we did not relocate.

Developing a deeper trust in God allows us to make peace with ourselves, knowing that all things work together for good for those who love God and are called according to His purpose (Romans

8:28). Nothing is wasted, not even the wrestling and searching for the right team. All of the conversations we have or relationships we have built throughout the years have been used by God to enable personal growth and development.

God is good. Psalm 34:8 tells us, "Taste and see that the Lord is good; blessed is the one who takes refuge in Him." It is in God's very nature to be faithful, and this comes down to the fact that He keeps His promises.

HOLD ON TO GOD'S PROMISES

God promises His people many things, and those promises apply to everyone, regardless of circumstances. I have chosen seven promises that I personally find helpful when I am struggling to trust God or feel like I am on a downward spiral towards hopelessness.

1. God is always with us.

People may come and go, relationships may fail, supports change or come to an end, but God promises to never leave us or forsake us (Hebrews 13:5).

2. God will protect us.

He wants what is best for us and He has our backs. If our lives are out of order and we are living our way instead of God's, we tend to attract trouble and strife. I encourage you to seek some counsel and prayer to work out where there is disorder. Then seek God and come back under His cover and protection (Psalm 91).

3. God is our strength.

He is likened to a strong tower that we can run to in troubled times. Other people in our lives may not always be able to offer the support and comfort we need in seasons of strife, but the Lord is our strength, and no matter how tough the situation, we can always lean on Him (Psalm 46:1; 61:3).

4. God will answer us.

He answers our prayers, He listens to what matters to our hearts, and He will lead and guide us along the pathway of life (Jeremiah 33:3).

5. God will provide for us.

He knows our needs and will provide, especially when we trust in Him for our provision. For example, God knew that we needed pets in our family, and He provided a supportive neighbour to assist us as a sponsor during financially tough times (Philippians 4:19).

6. God gives us His peace.

Even when life is in turmoil, we can know deep peace. We may not have all the answers. We may not understand why situations are as they are, but trusting in God always brings peace (John 14:27).

7. God will always love us.

We may not always feel lovable. We may have family members who are unable to demonstrate love towards us due to their own issues. But God's love is unconditional, He never stops loving us, and we can receive that love from Him (Psalm 103:17).

God's promises never fail. He has promised to love, guide, comfort and protect us, and I can testify to His faithfulness to keep His promises. I have had some low moments when I felt abandoned by God and couldn't see how situations could possibly work out. However, as I have come to Him with my pain and the impossible situations, He has not let me down. I do not always get my way, but when that is the case, I am learning to trust that there is a better plan. Others have observed this in my life—in fact, I have a friend who says, "If anyone can make it happen, Leisa can." I know it is not me who makes anything happen, but my God who loves and cares for me.

He knows us better than we know ourselves. So, I encourage you to pray with these promises in mind. It does not mean that your life will be perfect, but it does mean that you will not have to "go it alone.' God promises over and over in Scripture to be with you. He is your constant companion. He will walk with you through deep waters. He will lead you through both the good and bad times.

This is what it means to have a deeper trust in God. It is taking what God says about Himself in the Bible, trusting that it is true, and then being willing to apply it to your circumstances. Many people say that they believe what the Bible says. Perhaps they know the Bible well and have God's promises in their minds. However, when it comes to applying it to our own lives and circumstances, we need to go beyond simply knowing those promises. We need to have the courage to take a step of faith and trust that His promises are for us! They are for your circumstances, no matter who you are, wherever you live in the world and whatever has happened in your situation.

At first, trust may be challenging, especially if there is little, if any, obvious change to your circumstances. Remember, change begins from the inside out. As you become stronger and respond differently to events, a physical shift in outward circumstances occurs. Things start to fall into place or come together in ways that you might not expect.

In our case, I assembled a stable support team along with the resources I needed to help Justin navigate through his first eighteen years. Now, as he is transitioning from school into Bible college, I am starting that process again. A whole new set of challenges comes with this change. Without the school structure to support him, he will need full-time support while I am at work. We are at a crossroads again, and so we need to reapply the promises of God to our circumstances once more. If you are in a similar situation, ask yourself these questions:

How do God's promises apply to my circumstances?

Can I trust that God will come through?

What do I need to let go of so that I can trust God?

I will not deny that, with all the uncertainty that lies ahead, I have been battling anxiety once again. The 'what ifs' threaten to overwhelm me as I struggle to trust. However, I know deep down that this is actually an exciting place to be because, when I do not have the answers, God has an amazing opportunity to come through once again.

So, what *does* the future hold for Justin, me, Ian, and our other kids? I do not really know. I have glimpses of what it may look like. I have desires of what I would like it to look like. Still, ultimately, I trust in my Heavenly Father as to what it will be and I believe that His plans and purposes will surpass anything I could come up with on my own.

TRUST CULTIVATES HOPE

When we learn to trust in God more deeply and to believe that He is trustworthy and keeps His promises, there is hope! Hope and trust go hand in hand. If there is no trust, there is no hope. Both are optimistic feelings and emotions about the future, even when there is an unknown outcome. Trust is based on the reliability, confidence or belief in someone else, and for me, that someone else is God. Hope springs from trust.

Another Christian family I know with a similar situation to ours have also learned to trust in God, in spite of the disorder resulting from dysfunctional relationships and the challenges of special needs. I have seen them choose to trust that God will bring about healing and restoration in their children's lives. They committed to praying together for their kids each day, as well as doing everything they can to support them physically. At first, it seemed like nothing was changing. But their hope continues to rise little by little as they see each response to therapy. They have been encouraged as support teams have come together so they can take time out for a family picnic together. While this seems insignificant for ordinary families, an activity like this is a huge step forward for a special needs family.

It is their trust in God that enables them to persevere. It may seem slow, arduous, and never-ending, but if you stick with it, things will get better. No circumstances are too difficult for God. Scripture says, "Trust in the Lord with all your heart and lean not on your own understanding; in all your ways submit to him, and he will make your paths straight" (Proverbs 3:5-6).

Chapter Thirteen

Travelling the Pathway to Hope

Knowing God is ultimately what brings healing. It is intimacy with and surrender to God that will transform your life and bring about a shift in you and your loved ones. The question is whether you will trust God with healing for yourself and your child.

Every family's situation is unique. I do not know if God will bring about recovery in your family the way you hope for. I do know, however, that if you trust Him, He will bring about the transformation He knows is best for each of you. Building intimacy with Father God is essential if we are to walk into healing, and that intimacy is what ultimately builds hope. I discovered that putting my hope in a disability scheme, support workers or therapists, and even in significant others in my life did not fully work. At the end of the day, they are people too. They may have some solutions and be very helpful, but they do not have all the answers. In fact, no one does. Even God may not share with us all the answers we seek, and that is His prerogative. I have had to accept that some of my questions will remain unanswered, and that is okay! People, organisations, and even churches may let us down, but the fact remains that God will never let us down.

I am still on the journey of learning to trust, by the way! It is what underpins me in building a pathway to hope. When I began, my opinions as to how I should parent as a Christian mother were generally black and white. Yet, throughout the journey, I am becoming more and more unravelled as I yield to the more in-depth work of the Heavenly Father in my heart. This in no way minimises the truth of what I have shared in these pages. I am simply still learning and growing in grace in my walk with God!

The reality is that very little is black and white, and all truth needs to be shared in love. As Christians, we take the Word of God seriously. That means that we believe His Word does have answers and insights even for special needs families, and we find that the Bible can be a great source of comfort and strength. Some of its teachings may seem to be countercultural in our day and age, but this does not mean that those teachings are irrelevant. It is essential not to be heavy-handed when we talk about our faith, and so I say this lovingly: for genuine transformation to take place, we all need a more profound commitment to our walk with God. Unfortunately, many people's pain has gone unacknowledged or been brushed over, and as a result, some people discount the truth of Scripture. Sometimes the church has given a distorted perception of God. The sad reality is that many special needs families have felt so rejected, unloved and messy when they encounter a church environment that they may never return. It is important to keep in mind that most people do not know how to understand or relate to our lives. It is difficult to imagine or identify with the pain of others when it is so far removed from your own experience.

But people are never the real enemy. We all have an enemy called Satan, and he is very happy to portray Christians as hypocrites. He is glad for religion to be reduced to a set of rules that must be followed or service that must be completed to be accepted as part of the church family. This picture of religion leaves special needs families bound, feeling like it is an impossibility to keep up with the expectations of 'church'.

Therefore, the very people who most need connection with the Heavenly Father and His people struggle to consider drawing towards Him for comfort, healing and hope! Let's not confuse a relationship with God with a religious experience or church attendance. Religion is a man-made system that the enemy uses to keep people from connecting with the Father and receiving the comfort and hope that He longs to give. No matter the circumstances in your life, one step towards healing happens when we readjust the picture we have developed of God. If we are to allow Him to offer hope and bring healing, then revising our view of God is essential.

I actually came to a point where I entirely revaluated my faith and asked what I honestly thought and believed about God. I asked myself questions like:

- Are my circumstances too difficult for God?
- Can God make a way when there seems to be no way?
- Does God even care?
- How do I view God?
- Do I even believe the Bible when it says God works all things together for good?

You may need to grapple with these questions too, because it is your walk with God that will determine how you do or do not heal. For example, all the supports, tips and ideas suggested in the previous chapters will definitely help you make progress. There is no doubt about it, especially as much of it is backed by research and is evidence-based. But this is not an academic paper—it is an account of experience I have gained via the school of hard knocks! What I know is this: if you want more than a Band-aid over your circumstances, if you want a more permanent, lasting solution, it is worth discovering the heart of God. The healing He brings can contribute to recovery within your whole family unit.

ADDRESS THE DEEPER ISSUES

If you are willing to go deeper, it is worth identifying the circumstances that derail your comfort and security. We sometimes want to go back to a place in our lives where everything was 'perfect,' good and pain-free, when everything was more comfortable. It can be tempting to choose a pathway that offers a quick escape route. That escape route will look different for every person, but it may be something like a divorce, a hobby, working too many hours, or some type of addiction. Ask yourself where you seek comfort. What is your escape from the pressures of your life?

Ultimately, I had to learn to escape to the arms of Jesus, to run to Him for comfort, guidance and strength. It is in His presence that I can cry my tears, express my pain, tell Him my problems and *trust* that He can and will move the mountains in my life. There have been many mountains to climb, but with Him, I am climbing them *and* descending safely down the other side.

The mountains are not as hard to traverse now. I can testify to God's goodness and faithfulness. I know that just as He has come through before, He will come through for us again. For example, when I was transitioning Justin from early childhood education into school, we needed a whole new team to take him into the new season. It looked impossible, and I was stressed over figuring out who they would be. Yet, God was faithful and provided everyone and everything we needed for Justin's school years. Based on His past record, I can know that He will do it again.

WHEN PROBLEMS ARISE

Problems are inevitable in special needs families. However, when you choose to trust God, you have strategies for coping. Here is a simply pathway for finding resolution:

1. Bring the problem to God.
2. Do what you can do to resolve or move it forward.
3. Take your hands off the problem and trust God.
4. Lift the issue to God in prayer as He prompts you.
5. Do what God directs you to.

I am still working through how to avoid anxiety and trust more deeply in God, and I admit it is not easy. But if the Bible commands us not to worry, it must be possible. Ian also struggles, and we have sometimes had conflict between us when it comes to trusting in God for the future. He is a glass-half-empty kind of person. Therefore, as his wife, I have to take his concerns very seriously. What matters to him, matters to me. I don't want to rush over the issues with a "she'll be right, mate" attitude when it is genuinely hard to know if it will be, aside from God's supernatural power. This is why each person's individual healing journey is so crucial when it comes to cultivating hope.

I cannot force others to seek healing and restoration if they are not willing or ready. I can only acknowledge the hurt and pray that in time they will choose to release it all to God. It can be hard to be patient when longing for a certain outcome. Yet, as we keep our eyes on Christ, allow Him to work with us, and trust in His plans and purposes, it becomes easier to release our desires and trust Him.

How individuals respond to the challenges in special needs families is determined by our personal capacity to handle stress, what was modelled for us in our upbringing, and many other factors. There is no perfect way forward, and there are so many twists and turns that can divert our eyes from our goals. For these reasons and so many more, I have found that fixing my eyes on Jesus and finding hope in Christ is of vital importance.

Chapter Fourteen

———

Hope Wins

Ultimately, I have learned that whether hope wins in the end is not dependent on my circumstances. Hope does not depend upon whether my son is healed or whether everything lines up as I may have expected or even desired. When my life was turned upside down by Justin's diagnosis, it really rocked my world because I had firm ideas of what my life would be. What I have learned is that the journey towards renewed hope is key to who I am becoming. I know I can have joy despite my circumstances. Jesus is the cornerstone that holds my life together, and so I can experience peace even if there is turmoil and uncertainty around me.

I cannot separate my story from my faith in Christ. He is my hope. The process of deepening my faith in Christ has strengthened me in ways I could never have imagined. Just like the apostle Paul wrote about experiencing peace and joy even when he was in prison, I have learned that I can have peace regardless of my earthly circumstances.

Sometimes my life feels a bit like a prison. I still live with restrictions due to Justin's needs. I have not had the freedom to make choices like some others have in their lives, and I have had to make peace with that. The reality is that being a caregiver is an unpaid and often unacknowledged job, and few understand what it entails. That being said, much of my struggle came from deeper areas of brokenness in my life. As I uncovered ideas built on wrong mindsets and unhealthy patterns of relating, I became a much better person.

The apostle Paul said that whatever he thought he had gained was nothing compared to the worth of having a relationship with Christ. That relationship surpassed anything he may have once desired (Philippians 3:8). What is it that you once counted on? Is it an inheritance that will leave you debt-free, generational blessings of a strong family line, prosperity and a good life, your reputation or health? Christ is so much more than any of these things; the advantages gained on earth do not gain any advantage before God. It is His grace that sets us free, and we receive the gift of grace when we surrender our lives to Christ, asking Him to forgive our sins and take our pain, and trusting Him to lead our lives.

By not giving in to bitterness and self-pity and trusting Him in all circumstances, we receive hope in this life. We also have the hope of eternal life when every tear will be wiped away, and "there will be no more death or mourning or crying or pain, for the old order of things has passed away" (Revelation 21:4). Christians live their lives with the hope of eternity *and* the assurance that knowledge gives us while we are on earth.

But what about the pain and struggles we face in the here and now? The apostle Paul calls them 'light and momentary troubles' in 2 Corinthians 4:17. He had a long-term, eternal perspective! I know when I was in the height of my pain, my troubles felt neither light nor momentary but I chose to connect more deeply to God. As I learned to relate to Him as my Heavenly Father and deal with my baggage, my troubles did feel lighter. As I grew stronger, I came to see my situation not as a burden, but a blessing, because it brought me to the end of myself, and it was there that I indeed met Christ. Attending my retreat courses was key to moving through these painful times and to giving me hope that there would be change.

As I started to heal and respond to my circumstances in a healthier way, there was a spill-over effect into my family relationships. We are still a work in progress, but we are in a much better place than where we were. I take heart from others who have chosen to find hope in Christ amongst adverse situations, rather than setting their hope on science or psychology. While these do offer some answers and pathways for progress, in my personal experience and belief, they are not where hope is secured. Hope may be found in science for a season, but science is not ultimately what produces long-term, sustaining hope. Relying entirely on our own strength in complex or even everyday situations leads to feelings of hopelessness. Though there may be some relief while we are on earth, choosing to have faith and trust in Christ is what leads us into a deeper healing and restoration. It is in the moments when we 'let go and let God' that He turns up. Only Jesus Christ offers a hope which does not end.

Fanny Crosby was blind and yet she wrote over eight thousand hymns. She never gave in to bitterness and self-pity. In fact, she embraced her disability and thanked God for it because it drew her closer to Him. This woman is known to have said, "If perfect earthly sight had been offered to me, I might not have accepted it, as perhaps I would be distracted by all the sights and attractions I have never seen and not have sung praises to my God. My blindness has presented an opportunity for me to have a deep faith in God."

To seek Him first is paramount in all things. When life is turned upside down; our hope is in the Lord.

From birth, I took Justin to church and prayed for him. Shortly after his diagnosis, I had a time of prayer similar to that of Hannah in the Bible who was grieving over being barren. Like her, I brought my seemingly impossible situation intentionally before the Lord. Using the words of Hannah's prayer, I prayed over him as he slept. With many tears, I wept and promised God that if he healed and restored Justin's life and noticed my grief, I would raise Justin in the house of the Lord forever.

In one sense, this was not too different from our family's routine. We are regular church attenders, and the kids went to a Christian school. So, I didn't overthink what I had prayed once I had emotionally calmed down. Be intentional about what you pray! God obviously took my prayer very seriously. This is how my prayer has been answered over the years...

When Justin was in kindergarten, a guest speaker came, and Justin remembers responding to the invitation to give his life to Christ. As the years went by, Justin joined our church community, attended Christian studies classes at school, went on youth camps and even attended some Christian conferences, all fully supported. He was drawn to worship music and listened to it (and to the Christian radio station) every day.

When he was twelve, we were filling in paperwork for the National Disability Insurance Scheme, and when Justin was asked his goals, and he stated, "My goal is to be a pastor and go to Bible college." He told us that during a conference we had just attended, he felt called to be a pastor. This goal has never wavered over the years, and now we now find ourselves here. Justin has recently enrolled in Bible college online and is stepping towards his desire to be a pastor.

I have to be honest. At first, Ian and I wondered if it was an autistic obsession, like being fixated on cars. But the reality is that we have come to see that he is being drawn by God to serve Him in full-time ministry. Justin still hopes to attend as a full-time student on campus in the future and will volunteer in our church community as he transitions from school into the next season of his life. It gives us great hope as we watch God work out His plans and purposes in Justin's life amid the continued challenges, especially managing a tic disorder, which makes it difficult for him to be still and focus. We draw on the Scripture which says Justin can do all things through Christ who strengthens him (See Philippians 4:13). What looked hopeless to the medical professionals, and what appeared to be so much work that we could easily have given up before even starting is not an issue for God. As I watch my son's life, I am drawn into deeper faith and trust.

This story is unfolding as it is being written, so watch out for the next book. I love a happy ending, and I believe there will be one when I look back over my life. What that ending looks like, I do not precisely know, but God knows, and that is what counts. And that is where I have to put my hand in His and let Him guide me, waking each day to say, "What next, God?"

Learning to hear His voice as I connect with Him through His Holy Spirit is so important. This has been the key to knowing how to navigate my journey. I am uncertain as to what my future holds and there is the reality that I will continue to have to lay down many aspects of my life. For Justin to be where he feels called requires someone who cares 'a whole awful lot' to enable his hopes, dreams, call, and desires to happen. But with the Holy Spirit leading, I can trust that everything will come together one step at a time.

When we have strong desires placed deep within us, they are there for a reason, and I believe they are placed there by God. The Bible says in Psalm 37:4, "Take delight in the Lord, and he will give you the desires of your heart." Notice that it says God gives you the desires of your heart; He does not give you your heart's desire. Our hearts can desire some pretty nasty stuff, so what we think we want is not always from God. However, God does put desires deep in our heart. We can be sure that if those desires do not go away, they are most likely placed there by God. The desire Justin has to be a pastor has not gone away; it continues to grow, and he is determined by the grace of God to move through his obstacles to allow it to happen. This included having to complete an extra year of school, which he was not happy about but came to accept.

The reality is that this part of Justin's story is not entirely played out. If Justin's dream does not come to pass exactly as he desires, does that mean hope does not win? Of course not! When Justin's plans do not go as he hoped, he is learning to trust in God. Right now, he does not know if and when he will be able to attend classes on campus, but we are trusting God as to how it all unfolds!

For a very long time, I have had a desire to write books, teach and speak to help others along their journey. From the time I was a small child, I loved to read books and then spend hours telling Mum or anybody who would listen what I read. In our family, whenever one of us read a book, we would discuss the story and share a synopsis with another family member. Mum and Dad particularly liked reading autobiographies and were intrigued with other people's life stories. I think this showed me how people's stories, when shared, offer a great source of hope and encouragement, and my desire has been to provide that for others by sharing our family's story.

As I look back, I can see God's hand in developing my writing and my desire to write. Because of Justin's needs, I have had to spend more time at home than anticipated. I made a conscious choice to use my time wisely instead of giving in to self-pity. Over the years, I have written many courses, devotionals and curriculums for my work or Christian ministries in which I have been involved. God has used what I found to be a restrictive environment to further develop a desire that He placed in my heart. Therefore, my struggles are being used not only to give others hope, but also to give me hope that there is a unique purpose and plan for each and every one of our lives. If we take what is in our hands and allow ourselves to roll with our situation rather than resist it, good can come from it and we can become all that we are purposed to be. Then we are also able to assist in seeing those plans and purposes brought to fruition in the lives of our loved ones.

I believe many families are sacrificing greatly, whether because of high needs in their family, or even the increased demands of high-performing children. Huge sacrifices are made, for example, by parents of children who are training to become elite athletes. The dedication and financial cost to ensure our children succeed is often incalculable. But while these sacrifices are costly, they are not nearly as costly as the sacrifice made by Jesus when He laid down His life for us so that we no longer have to carry the burden of sin and pain. He did this so that our relationship with God could be restored and we could have direct access to the Heavenly Father. Because of His sacrifice, we can trust that He has us in His heart, that He wants the best for our lives, and that our loved ones are safe under His care and protection.

Our world is not in great shape. People are insecure, fearful and anxious about many issues. Jesus says in John 16:33, "I have told you these things, so that in me you may have peace. In this world you will have trouble. But take heart! I have overcome the world." It is freeing when we stop clinging to physical things to give us hope. People may still disappoint, words may hurt, attitudes may isolate and block us from achieving our goals, resulting in anger. However, when we come to know the One whose very nature is to give hope, the rest fades away. Hope in Christ builds character as we experience His faithfulness, which enables us to persist in the face of adversity.

The Bible talks about this when it says that our suffering produces perseverance; perseverance, character; and character, hope (Romans 5:3-4). All those years ago, I would not have thought that my journey of receiving the gift of a special needs son would also be about my character development. This change meant I learnt to trust that God is faithful, that all of His promises are true, that I can be quietly confident that God will be faithful to my family's needs and to me.

Experiencing God's repeated faithfulness throughout the trials and struggles in raising Justin has increased Ian's faith too. I have a habit of saying, "God has done it before, so He will do it again." Over and over, we have seen God's hand of mercy and grace upon our family. We do not deserve it, yet that does not stop God from offering mercy anyway. He not only gives us strength to climb the mountains we face—he moves mountains on our behalf. Every time we think there is no way forward, God makes a way, though it may not be what we anticipated or what we might choose. Still, because of His track record of opening doors and caring specifically for our needs as a family, we have learnt to trust that His way and timing is perfect.

Hope also wins as Justin's confidence and faith in God grow. He has so much untapped potential! When people slow down and take the time to see past the disability, they are amazed. The Bible says that "the Lord does not look at the things people look at. People look at the outward appearance, but the Lord looks at the heart" (1 Samuel 16:7). I thank God for all those people who have cared 'a whole awful lot' and taken the time to get to know Justin and in turn discovered his heart and love for Jesus and his desire to help others.

Finally, hope wins as we see that God has been Justin's refuge throughout the years, a strong tower of strength in the midst of the resistance he has faced enabling him to become who God has created him to be, a young man who loves God. And, hope wins as I too continue to find my refuge in Christ and become the woman that God has purposed and planned for me to be.

Therefore, it is with confidence that I can say, "Hope wins!" God always wins! He has a purpose and a plan, and He never leaves or forsakes us. He knows our needs, and He is a good God. We can trust in Him, no matter what our circumstances are. I look forward to writing future books to share how His plan further unfolds in our lives and to testify of God's grace in that continuing journey. It is my prayer that you will come to know the peace that passes all understanding as you fix your eyes on the one who is HOPE!

Author's Note

It was tempting to write a 'glory story' with glowing picture of my family standing victoriously on top of a mountain — an inspirational, self-help book that showed how we truly battled the odds and came out triumphant. A true before-and-after story. But that's not our reality, and it's not what I ultimately desire for my readers. Though there is truth in the saying "you have seen the glory but you don't know the story," as my readers, you have seen God's glory in my life *and* you now have a glimpse of the story!

My story is one of hope, and yet hope does not always mean healing. Living a meaningful life is not always what you envision it to be. There is a fine line between hope and healing because when we pray for 'healing' it often comes with a strong expectation of what that healing looks like. Sometimes it's physical — other times it's spiritual, or emotional, or relational.

For this reason, when I pray for Justin, I am asking that he will be all that God has made him to be. The Bible says that we are all made in the image of God. The differences in my son are what make him unique. His behaviour has been extremely challenging, but it is never too much for God, and the issues he deals with are not too complex for God. What I am convinced of is that God loves me and my family — and He loves yours just as much!

So, rather than praying for Justin to be healed of his disorder, I focussed on my own inner healing, on growing my relationship with my Heavenly Father and learning to trust in Him more deeply. That is why today I have real hope, whether my son or family are ultimately healed or not. Now I can confidently entrust every detail of my family's lives to Him, and as a result we have seen miracles happen! My son, who at the age of eighteen months was given a grim diagnosis that he would never be able to talk and would always have the mind of a baby, is now at Bible college and studying hospitality at a technical college.

If you have read my story but do not know Jesus, and would like to begin a journey of faith and trust in Him I encourage you to simply pray. Find a quiet place and pour out your heart to God in your own words. Tell him how hard it's been, and how you can't do it on your own. Ask him to uncover the grief you have been carrying, and allow him to forgive you for the ways you may have responded that have hurt yourself and those around you. As you ask Jesus into your life, ask Him to fill you with His Holy Spirit, and to empower you as you begin your journey with Him. You might like to use the words of the prayer below. Then seek out a Christian, or find a church nearby. Faith was never meant to be done alone! Just as we all need God, we all need each other! May God bless you, strengthen you, and fill you with hope!

> *Dear Jesus, thank you for loving me. I come to you because I need you in my life. I ask You, Jesus, to heal me, forgive me, restore me. Be my Lord and Saviour. Fill me with Your Spirit and lead me into hope, I pray. Amen.*

Acknowledgements

I have been enabled to write this book because many people who care 'a whole awful lot' have journeyed alongside me. Thank you all.

To Justin. Thank you, my wonderful son, for being willing to let me share our story. Our lives have been entwined far more than most mother-son relationships, and I am so proud of the man you are becoming. I look forward to releasing you towards more and more independence every day. I know God has amazing plans for your life!

To my family, and especially my husband Ian. Special thanks for allowing me to include your story with mine and thus make us all vulnerable in the hope that our lives might help others.

To my parents. Though far away, you always tried to do what you could to help out. Though Dad is no longer with us, his practical support was invaluable around the house. Thank you too, Mum. You always gave what you could when your own life was so busy.

To Andrew. I am grateful for a brother who encourages me to remain on the narrow path and never allows me to give up hope.

To Jenny Haines. Thank you for being my dear friend, intercessor and confidant. I am grateful for the countless hours you have spent in prayer and intercession, bringing our seemingly hopeless situations before God and celebrating our wins with me.

To Justin's therapy teams. Thank you for investing so much into Justin's life. I especially acknowledge Helen and Kam who never give up and have walked with us tirelessly throughout the years. Thank you, too, Helen, for your generosity in allowing me to use your HOPE acronym on the back cover.

To the support workers. My greatest thanks to Kylie, Jenny G, Narelle, Janet, Jane, Michael, Will, Jenny W, Gwenda, Tracey, Karen and countless others who have stood by us year in and year out and been prepared to go the extra mile to invest in Justin and provide us with the support we need as a family.

To Natalie Knill. As you watched my life you often wondered how I managed. It was your questions that first encouraged me to put my story into print. Thank you!

To Capital Edge Community Church. We are so grateful to you for accepting, loving and including us all. To Hamish and Meg, I'm especially grateful that you noticed Justin at youth group when he was younger and took the time to talk to him.

To the team at Ellel Ministries, Australia. Thank you for hosting the retreat weekends that began my healing journey. You have prayed, wept, and walked with me for many years and continue to do so. It is an honour to now join you in leading others into freedom and wholeness!

To Chris Conway. Thank you for running an amazing community gym. You have been a stabilising factor in my life and assisting with my health and wellbeing.

To Therese Ivey, who has helped us design all our home modifications. We would never have made it without you.

To Diana Bennett, our incredible neighbour. Your kindness and abundance of practical assistance and support with pets in times of great need will never be forgotten. We are also immensely grateful to **Assistance Dogs Australia** who placed our wonderful therapy pet with us when we were at a low ebb.

Though this is not a statement of political preference, I also wish to acknowledge former Prime Minister of Australia, **Julia Gillard**, who tackled the last frontier of human rights to raise the profile of the needs of people who live with disabilities. Thank you!

Leisa with her son, Justin

Follow our journey or get in touch at:

- leisawilliamsauthor.com
- @LeisaWilliamsAuthor

www.ingramcontent.com/pod-product-compliance
Lightning Source LLC
Chambersburg PA
CBHW031250290426
44109CB00012B/523